An Introduction to Wesleyan Theology

An Introduction to Wesleyan Theology

Revised and Enlarged Edition

by
William M. Greathouse
and
H. Ray Dunning

Beacon Hill Press of Kansas City
Kansas City, Missouri

Permission to quote from the following copyrighted versions of the Bible is acknowledged
with appreciation:
    The *New American Standard Bible* (NASB), © The Lockman Foundation, 1960,
1962, 1963, 1968, 1971, 1972, 1973, 1975, 1977.
    The *New English Bible* (NEB), © The Delegates of the Oxford University Press and
The Syndics of the Cambridge University Press, 1961, 1970.
    The Holy Bible, New International Version (NIV), copyright © 1973, 1978, 1984 by
the International Bible Society.
    The *Revised Standard Version of the Bible* (RSV), copyrighted 1946, 1952, © 1971,
1973.

10   9   8   7   6   5   4   3

Contents

Preface   7
Prologue—Revelation and the Bible   9

Part I—THE TRIUNE GOD

1 God   19
2 Jesus Christ   28
3 The Holy Spirit   39

Part II—MAN, SIN, AND GRACE

4 The Nature of Man   51
5 The Atonement   61
6 Divine Grace and Human Response   70

Part III—THE CHRISTIAN LIFE

7 Salvation   81
8 Sanctification   90
9 The Church   99
10 The Sacraments   107
Epilogue—The Return of Christ   117
Glossary   123
Bibliography   127
Subject Index   129
Person Index   131
Scripture Index   132

Preface

The content of this book has passed through several stages of development. The first stage was a series of expositions of Christian doctrine that appeared in the September/October/November 1977 edition of the Enduring Word Sunday School curriculum. These were written by Dr. Greathouse. Subsequently I took those brief summations and elaborated them to provide the first edition. That volume was titled, after the work was complete, *An Introduction to Wesleyan Theology.*

When considering the possibility of a second edition, it seemed appropriate to refocus some of the material to more accurately reflect the title. The first edition made considerable reference to the creedal statements of a particular Wesleyan denomination, which restricted its use somewhat. In order to make it usable by a wider audience, we decided to change that emphasis so that Wesleyans of whatever denominational affiliation (or none) could have an elementary study of their own larger tradition. In addition we have added a short list of appropriate sources at the end of each chapter to provide further reading for students who may be using the book as a text and desire broader study.

John Wesley was the human agent in a great spiritual movement in the 18th century commonly called the Evangelical Revival. His contribution to Christian spirituality produced a distinctive interpretation of the Christian faith that has attracted thousands of followers. It is, among other things, a perpetuation of the movement commonly associated with the name of James Arminius (Arminianism) and appropriates the best and most biblical insights of Roman Catholic thought, the Eastern Catholic tradition, and classical Protestantism.

Thus Wesleyan theology is no theological provincialism but is committed to the beliefs articulated by the ecumenical creeds of the first few centuries of the Christian era. It furthermore engages in dialogue with the major strands of the historic Christian faith, holding to no beliefs not solidly based in Scripture. Its primary

7

emphasis is on salvation and those beliefs that are "essential to salvation," that is, those that make salvation, broadly conceived, possible. This means that Wesleyan thought is not preoccupied with merely speculative matters.

This work, however, is not strictly a study of the theology of John Wesley as a historical figure. Rather, it takes the basic Wesleyan commitments and attempts, where appropriate and necessary, to state them in more contemporary terms than the 18th-century evangelist put them. It therefore draws upon recent developments in biblical studies, theological works, and philosophical ideas. This is precisely the ongoing task of theology, to state the meaning of the faith for each generation in terms of its own situation.

We hope that those who are in the various branches of the Wesleyan tradition will find this book helpful in understanding their own distinctive emphases in these days.

—H. RAY DUNNING

Prologue

Revelation and the Bible

Revelation is the theological term used to refer to God's self-disclosure to humankind. Man, by his own searching, cannot discover God. It is therefore necessary for God to make himself known if human beings are to have knowledge of Him. The fundamental conviction of the Christian faith is that this unveiling of the Divine has occurred in the person and work of Jesus of Nazareth. It recognizes that there were preliminary revelations to the Hebrews in epiphanies, theophanies, the law, and through prophets; but all these were preparatory to and reach their climactic fulfillment in Jesus (Heb. 1:1-3).[1]

Biblical faith is unique among world religions in believing that God has made himself known through historical events, notably the Christ-event. Hence Christianity is not primarily a system of ideas (i.e., a philosophy) but a commitment to a historical occurrence as the clue to the meaning of God, history, and human existence. This is why other religions would be unaltered if all relation to their founder was severed, but with Christian faith, severance from Jesus of Nazareth would result in annihilation.

Two major implications follow from this perspective: *First*, like all historical events, those that Christianity holds to be revelatory are accessed only by eyewitnesses. Those who are not eyewitnesses are dependent upon their reports for knowledge of these events. Furthermore, historical events are in need of interpretation for their significance to be known. Thus a claim that revelation has

---

1. For a distinction between an epiphany and a theophany as revelatory phenomena, see Claus Westermann, *Elements of Old Testament Theology*, trans. Douglas W. Stott (Atlanta: John Knox Press, 1982), 25-27.

9

occurred in a historical event needs both a report of the event and an interpretation of it. In the light of this, contemporary biblical scholarship views the Bible as the Book of the "mighty acts of God" (Ps. 106:2; 145:4, 12; 150:2; cf. Deut. 11:7; Judg. 5:11; 1 Sam. 12:7; Acts 2:22; 3:12-26) along with a Spirit-inspired interpretation (2 Pet. 1:16-21).

The implication of this perspective is that the Scriptures become the primary medium through which we have access to revelation and those truths that may accompany it. In that sense, Scripture is an aspect of revelation itself.

Second, while revelation involves an intellectual content, being a Christian does not consist in believing those truths that make up the network of Christian beliefs. Rather the Scripture is the means by which one, in faith, enters into a life-transforming relation to the God who has disclosed himself in the events to which the Bible bears witness.

This truth stands behind Wesley's famous declaration:

> I want to know one thing—the way to Heaven; how to land safe on that happy shore. God Himself has condescended to teach the way; for this very end He came from heaven. He hath written it down in a book. O give me that book! At any price, give me the book of God! I have it: here is knowledge enough for me. Let me be *homo unius libri* [man of one book].[2]

This means that the Bible itself is not an object of faith. God alone is the proper object of saving faith. To elevate the Bible to the status of an object of worship would be idolatry (bibliolatry).[3] It should be recognized for what it is, the record of the divine self-disclosure. We trust the veracity of Scripture and believe it on the basis of the self-authenticating character of its message. This is what theologians refer to as the internal testimony of the Holy Spirit (*internum testimonium Spiritus Sancti*).

It is significant that no reference to the Bible is found among the faith commitments of the creeds of the ecumenical church (Nicea, Ephesus, Constantinople, Chalcedon, et al.). But the faith that is confessed there is validated by the authoritative word of Scripture even though the forms of expression are drawn from contemporary philosophical categories (nature, person, hypostasis,

---

2. *Standard Sermons*, ed. Edward H. Sugden, 2 vols. (London: Epworth Press, 1921), 1:31-32.

3. See H. Orton Wiley, *Christian Theology*, 3 vols. (Kansas City: Nazarene Publishing House, 1940-43), 1:36-37.

ousia, etc.). This should suggest the proper role of Scripture among essential beliefs.

What does it mean to refer to the 66 books of our Bible as *Holy* Scripture? William Barclay says the word *holy* means "different." God alone is holy in the absolute sense: He is unique, in a category to himself, qualitatively different from all He has created. The Bible is holy in the sense that it is different from all other books, in a category to itself, revealing the Holy One in a unique way. But its holiness is derivative, not inherent. If God alone is holy in the absolute and underived sense, the adjective *holy* is applied to the Bible in terms of its message and is thus derived from the One to whom it bears witness.

Inspiration of Scripture

In biblical usage, "word" and "work" in relation to God are synonymous. As the Word of God, the Scripture is essentially "salvation history," a fully trustworthy account of God's saving acts, which find their fulfillment in Jesus Christ. Prophets and apostles were called and given a unique inspiration to record and interpret God's saving acts in our behalf. The authority of the Bible is to be posited on these grounds.

Two passages in the New Testament refer to the "inspired" character of the Old Testament writings, and we may with justification now refer it to New Testament writings: "All scripture is given by inspiration of God, and is profitable for doctrine, for reproof, for correction, for instruction in righteousness: that the man of God may be perfect, throughly furnished unto all good works" (2 Tim. 3:16-17). "Knowing this first, that no prophecy of the scripture is of any private interpretation. For the prophecy came not in old time by the will of man: but holy men of God spake as they were moved by the Holy Ghost" (2 Pet. 1:20-21).

Wesleyans usually refer to the inspiration of Scripture by using the term *plenary*. This term means "full," as when we speak of a plenary session of a legislative body, that is, when all members are present. It is sometimes used to imply that the Holy Spirit's inspiration extends to the *full* canon of the Old and New Testaments. This involves the belief that the same Spirit who moved upon the authors of the Bible guided the Jewish church in selecting as authoritative the holy writings that now comprise the 39 books of our Old Testament and that He also guided the Christian

Church in recognizing as Holy Scripture the 27 books of our New Testament.

The method by which the Spirit inspired the Scripture has been interpreted by Wesleyans in different ways. The Bible itself gives little clue to this matter except to affirm that Scripture is inspired ("God-breathed" [2 Tim. 3:16, NIV]) and thus not written as a private or individual endeavor (see 2 Pet. 1:21). This leaves the Christian scholar free to explore all possibilities that do not conflict with any facts in the case. He is bound only to carry on his work *under* the authority of the Scripture.

The majority of Wesleyan scholars today appear to support the position that the inspiration and authority of Scripture extends to those truths necessary to salvation but not necessarily to scientific, historical, and other nontheological matters.[4] To go beyond this would be to claim more than can be justified. The Bible is not a book of science or a secular history, it is a Book of God—that is, its authoritative pronouncements are theological in nature.

The inspiration of the Bible is not to be compared with the inspiration of other great literature. It is not the product of human genius but of divine initiative. "God hath spoken" to us in the Bible, disclosing to us His heart and purposes. He so actuated, guided, and controlled the human authors and compilers of the Bible by the Holy Spirit that their writings have become for us His very written Word.

The significance and function of Holy Scripture can be grasped through an analysis of three affirmations, all of which are necessary to a full-orbed understanding of the Bible: (1) The Holy Scriptures *are* the written Word of God; (2) they *contain* the Living Word of God; and (3) they *become*, for those who have faith, the personal Word of God.

Holy Scripture Is the Written Word

What does it mean to refer to the Bible as the Word of God? How is it possible to use this language? Certainly it cannot be claimed that the whole Bible contains the words of God. There are Temple

---

4. Larry Shelton, "John Wesley's Approach to Scripture in Historical Perspective," *Wesleyan Theological Journal* 16, no. 1 (Spring 1981): 23-50; W. T. Purkiser, et al. *Exploring Our Christian Faith*, rev. ed. (Kansas City: Beacon Hill Press of Kansas City, 1978), 65-66; etc.

records, prayers of men, pronouncements of prophets, and even words from the devil; and these examples only scratch the surface of the almost infinite variety of materials. How are we to explain the designation "Word of God" as applied to the Bible?

An important distinction must be made between the word of God (lowercase) and the Word of God (uppercase). The latter comes to expression in the former, making the former the vehicle of God's self-communication. It is critically important for there to be an objective point of reference. Without that it would be too easy to confuse the Word of God with subjective feelings. But the words of Scripture provide a benchmark by which to constantly check the authenticity of our claims to hearing the Word of God.

It is possible to accurately understand the words of Scripture without ever hearing the word of God. In that sense the two can never be equated. Nonetheless, the Word is heard through the words and cannot be separated from them without serious danger. In that case, as W. T. Purkiser has quipped, "The inner light is the surest road to outer darkness." Because of its necessary function of mediating God's self-disclosure to humankind, the Bible can legitimately be referred to as "the Word of God."

Holy Scripture Contains the Word of God

We do not know what the Bible is unless we recognize its ultimate purpose: that is, to preach Christ as Savior and Lord. Martin Luther spoke of Holy Scripture as the cradle in which Christ may be found. We can become preoccupied with the hay and straw of the cradle if we choose, and become utterly confused and lost in the process. But if we permit the Spirit to guide us as we read and study the Book, our concentrated gaze will fall upon Christ!

By forgetting that Christ is King of Scripture (*Christus regnum scriptura*) and that the divine intention behind the Bible is to reveal Him, we may substitute the written Word for the Living Word. This is to force the written Word into the false position mentioned above. H. Orton Wiley gave this caution when referring to some in a previous century: "Men's knowledge became formal rather than spiritual. . . . They gave more attention to creeds than to Christ. . . . The Bible thus divorced from its mystical connection with the Personal Word became in some sense a usurper, a pretender to the throne."[5]

---

5. *Christian Theology* 1:142.

The Bible then *contains* the Living Word, Christ. "You diligently study the Scriptures because you think that by them you possess eternal life," Jesus said to the Pharisees, and added: "These are the Scriptures that testify about me" (John 5:39, NIV). After the Resurrection He chided two of His own disciples, "'How foolish you are, and how slow of heart to believe all that the prophets have spoken! Did not the Christ have to suffer these things and then enter his glory?' And beginning with Moses and all the Prophets, he explained to them what was said in all the Scriptures concerning himself" (Luke 24:25-27, NIV). We do not read the Scriptures aright, even the Old Testament of which Jesus spoke, unless we find in them the saving testimony to Christ (cf. 1 Pet. 1:10-12).

Holy Scripture May Become God's Personal Word

In the community of faith God *uses* Scripture as the chosen method of communicating himself and His will, so that we may understand our identity and vocation as the people of God, and receive guidance on how we are to live, act, and worship. God's use of the Bible, however, becomes effective only through the illuminating activity of the Spirit.

The proper attitude to assume, therefore, in reading the Bible is that of the child Samuel who was instructed by Eli to answer, "Speak, Lord; for thy servant heareth" (1 Sam. 3:9). We must be silent and receptive before the Scripture, eager and responsive to what the Spirit would say to us in its pages.

We must learn to *attend* God's Word in Scripture. When our reading is thus listening to God, Holy Scripture *becomes* God's personal word of promise, or rebuke, or counsel, or comfort, or whatever it is He sees we need. To pray as we read, and read as we pray—this is the proper approach to Holy Scripture. Suddenly a familiar verse flames with new meaning as the Spirit illuminates it to our hearts!

Over the years our personal Bibles take on very sacred meaning, for throughout their pages we pen our notes of praise where God has spoken to us in a moment of illumination. Promises God has given and fulfilled we have noted. How precious the Book of God becomes to one who has learned to hear within it the speaking voice of the Lord! "Man shall not live by bread alone, but by every word that proceedeth out of the mouth of God" (Matt. 4:4).

"The Book, the Book, bring me the Book!" the dying Sir Walter Scott said to a servant.

"What book, sir?" he asked.

Scott's answer is one every believer can understand. "There is only one Book, the Book of God!"

Theological Use of the Bible

In addition to these affirmations, the Bible also provides the raw material for theology. As has been noted, Scripture functions primarily as witness to God's saving work in Christ to bring us to Him and apprise us of the implications of that encounter for life. But belief is also an important part of religion although second in priority to the existential dimension.

As a source for doctrine, the Bible does not contain many theological propositions, although there are some.[6] However, a theological understanding informs every biblical passage. It is the task of the biblical exegete to bring this to light; it is the task of the theologian to incorporate these insights into doctrinal formulations to guide the beliefs and practices of the church.

The theologians of the church have worked at this task from the very beginning of the Christian era. The results of their work constitute the history of Christian thought. Each age has attempted to express the biblical truth in terms of its own day and age, to bring the resources in the Scripture to bear on its particular problems. This is still the work of the theologian today; and in doing this, he draws not only on Scripture as his authoritative Source but also upon the work of his predecessors for guidance, although he is constantly bringing their conclusions to the Scripture for final validation. In a word, the truth of Scripture is the reviewing stand before which all doctrinal statements must pass for judgment. It is this method that the authors of this introductory study of some foundational Christian beliefs interpreted from the Wesleyan perspective have sought to employ. By intention, they have placed themselves *under* the authority of the Word, both Living and written.

---

6. W. T. Purkiser, et al., *God, Man, and Salvation: A Biblical Theology* (Kansas City: Beacon Hill Press of Kansas City, 1977), 18-19.

Suggested Additional Reading

Robert D. Branson, *God's Word in Man's Language.*

F. F. Bruce, *The Books and the Parchments.*

Ralph Earle, "Revelation and Inspiration," *A Contemporary Wesleyan Theology* 1:287-326.

God's Word for Today, ed. Wayne McCown and James E. Massey, vol. 2 of *Wesleyan Theological Perspectives.*

I. Howard Marshall, *Biblical Inspiration.*

Alan Richardson, *The Bible in the Age of Science.*

PART **I**

The Triune God

God

Not every religion necessarily believes in God. However, for the Christian faith, such a belief is foundational. If there is no God, every facet of the Christian religion collapses as mere fanciful speculation. Thus it is our initial commitment and firm conviction that *God is*.

God's Existence

How do we know that God is? Properly, this is not really a theological question, since theology proceeds on the accepted premise of God's existence without making any attempt to prove it. The Bible itself makes no explicit reference that could be construed as an argument for the reality of the Divine. Gen. 1:1 reflects the biblical perspective on this matter: "In the beginning God . . ." Ps. 14:1 (repeated in Ps. 53:1) seems to hint at the possibility of denying the existence of God. But some of the newer translations, such as the *New English Bible,* as well as the immediate context suggest that this is more of a practical atheism: "The impious fool says in his heart, 'There is no God.'" The immoral man's behavior reflects a practical denial of God; that is, he is living as if there were no God.

The question of God's existence is more properly a question for students of the philosophy of religion, since that discipline tests the affirmation of faith at the bar of critical reason.

But within this context, certainly belief in God is not contrary to reason, as the history of philosophy illustrates. In the pre-Socratic period, the earliest Greek philosophers attempted to discover the ultimate world-stuff, or the basic ingredient(s) out of which everything was made. They suggested first a single element such as water (Thales) or fire (Heracleitus), and later multiple elements such as earth, air, fire, and water (Empedocles) or an infinite number of elements (Anaxagoras). But further reflection led Anaxagoras to the introduction of mind (nous) as the principle of intelligent direction and evolvement. His predecessors had struggled to provide a principle of change but had failed to find a satisfactory solution to the problem. In suggesting the divine Mind as the explanation of this enigma, Anaxagoras developed the first philosophic conception of God. This is what Aristotle called a deus ex machina (God outside the machine). Thus he reflects the recurring inclination of philosophers to identify as Deity the highest conception their theories had led them to use for explaining the world.

Eventually the idea of God as the Soul and Prime Mover of the universe emerged in the thought of Plato and Aristotle. Plato, in his *Timaeus,* posited the existence of God (which he called a Demiurge) as a kind of divine architect to account for the present form of the world as we experience it. This is an early version of what has been classically called the cosmological argument for God's existence. Aristotle likewise posited the existence of God (which he called the Unmoved Mover) as a metaphysical principle of explanation to account for change in the world. In his system God moves the world, without himself being moved or changed. Such a God is a far cry from the biblical picture of the God who acts and loves, but it nevertheless shows how reason may point to an Ultimate Reality.

Modern philosophy, since the work of David Hume and Immanuel Kant, has taken a dim view of the possibility of "proving" the existence of God. Human reason, they argued, is incapable of dealing with God in the same way that it deals with objects of our experience such as tables and chairs. Christian theologians generally concur with these conclusions, and whereas theology books of a few generations ago would begin with a section dealing with philosophical arguments for God, a competent contemporary approach to theology would not utilize those so-called classical arguments as a foundation for doing theology. Nonetheless, Kant did, in fact, posit God's existence as a postulate of "practical reason." While it is true, then, that human reason is not antithetical to faith, it cannot establish faith with coercive proofs.

The apostle Paul recognized this, for in 1 Cor. 1:21 he wrote: "The world by wisdom knew not God." Neither the philosophers nor we know God due to reason having demonstrated His existence. We know Him because He has chosen to reveal himself to us. This self-disclosure takes place first at a subcognitive level in the form of a general awareness of an infinite dimension within our finite existence. It is this "sense of the numinous" (Rudolf Otto) that is the source of the universal phenomenon of religion. It is this aspect of human experience to which Paul points in his address on Mars' Hill (Acts 17). "Men of Athens, I perceive that in every way you are very religious. For as I passed along, and observed the objects of your worship, I found also an altar with this inscription, 'To an unknown god.' What therefore you worship as unknown, this I proclaim to you. The God who made the world and everything in it" (vv. 22-24, RSV).

To this awareness of God as the Eternal Presence, theologians give the term *general revelation*. Even the philosophers who posit God as the product of their rational activities are witnessing to this general revelation, since it is God's disclosing himself to their questing minds that is the basis of their "knowledge" of Him. All this is saying that there is no knowledge of God apart from revelation or self-disclosure. The Wesleyan attributes this universal knowledge of God to the activity of "prevenient grace."

General revelation, however, is not adequate, and therefore the Hebrew-Christian faith affirms that God has gone beyond this to what is commonly called *special revelation*. This form of revelation, from the biblical point of view, occurs in history, that is, through historical events, what the Scriptures call the "mighty acts" of God.[1] Although God has chosen to show himself in several events recorded in the Old Testament, the Christian faith holds that the final and decisive self-disclosure of God has taken place in the Christ-event (Heb. 1:1-3). Philosophy may respond to our

---

1. While the biblical revelation contains far more than the record of events and their interpretation, such events seem to be the point of reference for other forms of revelation, all of which are directly related to history. One exception to this principle is the Wisdom literature (Proverbs, Ecclesiastes, etc.), which is the wise man's distilled wisdom derived from long experience. It is best characterized as a "creation theology." In a word, despite a great variety of forms, God's self-disclosure is centrally rooted in history, and this sets biblical faith apart as unique among world religions.

awareness of God in universal human experience, but only in God's self-disclosure do we have a true knowledge of God's being and nature. As we have already observed, this full and final divine self-disclosure has occurred in Jesus Christ.

Furthermore, it is through the people of God that we today have access to this revelation. The revelation began millennia ago when the Lord called Abraham, entered into covenant with him, and then, in fulfillment of His promise to him, brought into existence the people of Israel. Through this people, God sent His Son, in whom He reconstituted Israel as the Body of Christ, made up of all who believe, both Jews and Gentiles (Eph. 2:11-22; 1 Pet. 2:9-10). We know who God is because of the witness of His people (both the old Israel and the new Israel) through the centuries. Because the Church has brought us the gospel, we have believed on and received Christ through the Spirit—and thus know God.

God's Nature

Many feel that the question of God's nature is more important than the question of His existence. Most people believe in a god of some sort; but from the Christian perspective, it is crucial to understand what God is like, since from this flows both worship and life.

As noted above, the God of the philosophers is more of a theoretical concept, a principle of explanation, an idea. By contrast the God of the Bible, the Father of our Lord Jesus Christ, is a personal Spirit who loves us and personally involves himself in our lives. But it is the same God about which both speak.

In the beginning, the nature of God was conveyed by means of the revelation of His name, since in biblical times, one's nature was often understood to be represented in his name. This is the deeper significance of the Divine Wrestler's question to Jacob, "What is thy name?" (Gen. 32:27). When Jacob, by speaking his name, confessed himself to be a cheat and a fraud, he was in a position to have his character (and name) changed: "Your name shall no more be called Jacob, but Israel, for you have striven with God and with men, and have prevailed" (v. 28, RSV).

God made himself known to Abraham by the name of El Shaddai (the Almighty God): "When Abram was ninety-nine years old the Lord appeared to Abram, and said to him, 'I am God Almighty; walk before me, and be blameless'" (Gen. 17:1, RSV). The call to "be thou perfect" (KJV) was prefaced by the disclosure of the character of the Deity making the call. This would give Abram the confidence that the divine power was available to him to enable him to achieve the goal. God Almighty was placing the whole power of creation in the service of Abraham's moral development.

The definitive name for God in the Hebrew faith came later, however, as God spoke to Moses at the burning bush and revealed the name of YHWH to him: "This is my name for ever, and thus I am to be remembered throughout all generations" (Exod. 3:15, RSV). It is an enigmatic name, the exact meaning of which scholars debate. It is variously translated "I am that I am," or probably more correctly, "I will be what I will be" (v. 14, RSV margin). In either case, Old Testament scholars are in general agreement in recognizing that it does not imply static being, changelessness. To interpret it in that way, as many have done, is to impose a Greek view of God upon it rather than a Hebrew view. In line with the biblical mode of revelation (through historical events) it may imply, "You will know Me to be what I show myself to be through My activity." YHWH is a God who acts, who participates in history. It is here that the contrast between the god of the philosophers and the God of the Bible becomes most vivid. It is with this in mind that the most characteristic way of referring to the Lord by the biblical writers is as "the living God."

In the oldest Hebrew writings God's name was spelled simply YHWH (technically called the *tetragrammaton*). The word was pronounced Yahweh. In time the sacred name became so revered that it was not permitted to be spoken. So another word meaning "Lord" was written above YHWH, the word "Adonai," to be spoken by the reader instead of the sacred name. In the Middle Ages when scholars began to study the ancient manuscripts again, they were confronted with a puzzle: Adonai always above YHWH. They solved the problem by combining the consonants of YHWH with the vowels of Adonai.[2] The result of this confusion was the hybrid word "Yahoway" or "Jehovah." We now know, however, that the correct name of God is Yahweh, sometimes spelled Jahvey (since *Y* and *J*, *w* and *v* are interchangeable letters). The important thing to remember is that this sacred name reveals God's nature, God present with His people as the One who is always adequate to every situation.

---

2. Hebrew does not have vowels, but these were provided by the medieval scholars known as the Masoretes, who produced the Masoretic text, which became the basis for much Bible translation.

Knowledge of God is not merely an intellectual matter but involves a call to commitment. For modern science the ideal of knowledge is detachment, whereas for the Hebrew it was union with the object of cognition. To know means to enter into most personal relations with, as is reflected in the biblical use of "know" to refer to the sexual union between a man and a woman. Furthermore to know God in the biblical sense is to know oneself. It is for this reason that Wright and Fuller can say, "Knowledge, then, is not of God's eternal being but of his claim upon us. . . . Man has knowledge only when he obeys, only when he acts in obedience."[3]

The Holy One

There arose in Israel an understanding of Yahweh quite unusual in the ancient world. Unlike the people around them, the people of the Lord came to view their God as alone, God. For their contemporaries it was a simple matter to add another god to an already well-populated pantheon, and no one was upset—not even the other gods. But this would never do in Israel, since Yahweh would allow no rivals. Any pretenders would only be impostors anyway, since only Yahweh was God. The term "holiness" is used to refer to this characteristic. God is unique, in a category by himself; He is the Holy One.

The basic meaning of holiness relates to what some have called God's "Godness." Its root meaning was "separateness"; and when applied to Yahweh, it sets Him apart from all that is finite and created. It stands for His transcendence and authenticates His claim to exclusive loyalty and worship. The gods in a polytheistic system may share devotion with each other because they do not lay claim to ultimacy. Yahweh, however, is a jealous God who will not share His glory with another (see Joshua 24).

Herein lies the heinousness of man's sin in the Garden. It was an attempt to become God, to deny the essential distinction between the Creator and the creature (see Rom. 1:18-25). God is GOD. We must "let God be God!" To refuse to acknowledge God as absolute is *the* sin. To acknowledge His sovereignty over our existence is to recognize His holiness.

While holiness belongs primarily or originally to God, it may

---

3. G. Ernest Wright and Reginald Fuller, *The Book of the Acts of God* (Garden City, N.Y.: Doubleday, 1960), 24.

be conveyed to man so that he too becomes holy, but in a secondary sense. As we acknowledge His claims upon us and freely submit to them, we become His property, separated to Him—holy. This possibility, however, depends upon a prior act of redemption on God's part, because through the Fall we become sin's slaves and now cannot free ourselves to give ourselves away. *God must redeem us before we can become holy.* Ancient Israel was redeemed by God's mighty act at the Exodus. This became the basis for the divine imperative to holiness. It is for this reason that the Decalogue begins, "I am the Lord your God, who brought you out of the land of Egypt, out of the house of bondage. You shall have no other gods before me" (Exod. 20:2-3, RSV).

This is the background of the command, "Ye shall be holy: for I the Lord your God am holy" (Lev. 19:2). To be holy is to be wholly yielded to God's sovereign will and obedient to His law. In New Testament terms it is to love God with all your heart and your neighbor as yourself, for love is the very essence of God's law (Matt. 22:34-40), which implies being saved from "*the* sin" of self-sovereignty.

God's holiness is thus not merely one characteristic among others. It is God himself making an absolute claim upon our obedience and trust, and sanctifying us as we yield to His sovereign Lordship.

The Sufficient One

This understanding of God's holiness leads logically to the conclusion that He is the Source of all that is. "In the beginning God created the heaven and the earth" (Gen. 1:1). All beings have dependent existence upon Him who is the Ground of their being. The implication of this is that God is independent of all things, being completely self-contained and therefore having need of nothing. This is Paul's announcement to the Athenians (Acts 17:[24-]25): "Neither is [he] worshipped with men's hands, as though he needed any thing."

This is doubtless the deeper significance of the use of plural terms in the Genesis account of creation. The name Elohim (plural) is ascribed to the Creator, and He is referred to by plural pronouns. Obviously Moses had no inkling of the Trinity, but he did understand the theological truth of God's "fullness of being" and self-sufficiency and attempted to express it by referring to the "social nature" of the Lord. Later on, as the Early Church experienced God in the person of Jesus Christ, the truth of the Trinity came to light as a more precise expression of this sufficiency.

The biblical picture of God at this point provides us with a clue to a proper understanding of creation. There is a popular explanation of the "why" of creation that sees God creating out of an incompleteness of being: He has a psychological need for companionship in order to be happy and so creates a being with whom He can find the fulfillment of this need. But as the Holy One, God is complete in himself. He does not need the world in order to be happy. He does not need anything we can do for Him. He does not need man. He does not need *anything*.

Creation, then, is a manifestation of God's fullness rather than His lack. Out of His bounty He makes all things. The finite universe is the expression of His infinite creativity. The overflowing of God's nature in creation is a foundational truth that finds its fullest expression in the exciting truth that

God Is Love

The holiness of God is the heart of the Old Testament revelation. The love of God is the heart of the New Testament disclosure. But everything hinges on the meaning of this love as a manifestation of God's essential nature. The New Testament writers picked up on a word that had previously not been widely used and employed it to describe God's distinctive type of love: *agape*. Unlike the word *eros*, which is love out of need; or *philia*, which extends love to the attractive object and desirable person, *agape* reaches out from fullness. God's love is based, not in the loveliness of the person loved, but in His own nature. It is the divine self-giving.

The most decisive manifestation of God's love is in the gift of His Son for our salvation. "In this was manifested the love of God toward us, because that God sent his only begotten Son into the world, that we might live through him" (1 John 4:9). Paul underscores this truth, reiterating it three times in Romans 5 (NIV): "When we were still powerless, Christ died for the ungodly" (v. 6); "God demonstrates his own love for us in this: While we were still sinners, Christ died for us" (v. 8); "When we were God's enemies, we were reconciled to him through the death of his Son" (v. 10).

In the final analysis, the God of the Christian faith is the very God who encounters us in the person of Christ. There is no other

God than the One who showed us His face and His heart in the Cross. H. Orton Wiley once raised the question, "What would happen if all the attributes of God were brought into play at one time?" Answer: the cross of Christ, where "love and faithfulness meet together; righteousness and peace kiss each other" (Ps. 85:10, NIV).[4]

Suggested Additional Reading

John Baillie, *Our Knowledge of God.*
H. H. Farmer, *Toward Belief in God.*
Nels F. S. Ferré, *The Christian Understanding of God.*
J. Kenneth Grider, "The Holy Trinity," *A Contemporary Wesleyan Theology* 1:375-409.
J. B. Phillips, *Your God Is Too Small.*
Albert Truesdale, "Theism," *A Contemporary Wesleyan Theology* 1:107-48.
Morris A. Weigelt, "God," *Beacon Dictionary of Theology,* 236.
J. S. Whale, *Christian Doctrine,* chap. 1.

---

4. See *Christian Theology* 2:285-86.

Jesus Christ

The commitment of the Christian faith concerning our knowledge of God is that He has fully and decisively revealed himself in Jesus Christ. The question of the person of Christ thus becomes a crucial element in the doctrinal structure of Christianity. Much of Christian thought is concerned with this issue.

One could even say, without much oversimplification, that the question that informs all New Testament theology is "Who is Jesus?" If one were to add to that the question "What was His work?" he would undoubtedly have all the substance of the New Testament. These two questions embody the theological doctrines known as Christology and the Atonement.

The answer to the first of these two crucial questions is given in the primary documents chiefly in terms of titles and images drawn from the Old Testament. This is especially true in the Synoptic Gospels (Matthew, Mark, and Luke), which seem to reflect the earliest strata of Christian understanding as well as Jesus' own self-understanding. As the Church spread into the Hellenistic world, certain other titles seemed to become more appropriate to say who Jesus was, and so we find different emphases developing.

In these Gospels, Jesus is referred to as Messiah, the Prophet, the Son of God, Servant, and by a title found almost exclusively on His own lips: Son of Man. All these titles reflect the conviction that Jesus was the Fulfillment of all the hopes and promises of Old

Testament faith. He was the "Seed of the woman," whose heel was bruised by the serpent's head (cf. Gen. 3:15). He was the King whose birth had been anticipated by the golden-tongued Isaiah (cf. 9:6). But foremost among all, He was the Suffering Servant in whose vicarious death "the Lord hath laid on him the iniquity of us all" (53:6). The foundation stones of Christology are thus found in the Old Testament, and it was from it that the apostles preached that Jesus was the promised Lord and Christ (see Acts 2:22-36).[1]

There is no neat separation in the New Testament itself between the person and work of Christ. The question "Who is Jesus?" is addressed in terms of what He does. This approach is commonly called a *functional* Christology. In later theological discussion, a distinction came to be made between the two, and the person of Christ became a separate subject for discussion chiefly in onto-logical rather than functional terms. These inquiries came to be dominated by cosmological concerns,[2] and consequently the pre-incarnate Christ came to be identified with the Logos.

The term *Logos* had a long and illustrious history, having appeared in the philosophy of Heracleitus in the sixth century B.C. and later in the teaching of the Stoics. For both the meaning was generally the same. It referred to the structure of the universe or the reason that informed reality. The point was that reality was not chaotic and disordered but ordered and purposeful. Consequently, there was meaning and value because there was purpose. It seemed only natural for Christian thinkers to suggest that in Jesus the purpose and meaning of the universe had come to expression in concrete human form. If one wanted to know what reality was like, he could find out by looking at Jesus, for here the structure of reality had become localized in a temporal, historical event. Life could only find meaning in Him.

The continuing discussion focused on the status and/or origin of the Logos. There were several early Christian thinkers who spoke of the Logos as having come into being as the creation of

---

1. For a full development of all the Christological titles see Oscar Cullmann, *The Christology of the New Testament,* trans. Shirley C. Guthrie and Charles A. M. Hall (Philadelphia: Westminster Press, 1959).

2. This concern arose under the influence of Hellenistic philosophy, which posited a great gulf between God and the world. God was viewed as too transcendent to either have created the world or entered history. Intermediary beings were conceived as being the agents of creation and doing the work of God on the earth. One of these inter-mediaries was called the Logos in some systems.

God—"His only begotten Son"[3] (John 3:16)—for the purpose of creating the world. This teaching did not arouse a great deal of opposition until it was given expression by a presbyter named Arius.

The teaching of Arius became the subject of discussion and debate that finally culminated in the Council of Nicea that convened in A.D. 325. In the course of the deliberation, Arianism (the teaching that the Logos was a created being and so not coeternal with God) was condemned as heresy, and the orthodox Christian view was embodied in the famous Nicene Creed:

> We believe in one God, the Father Almighty, Maker of all things, both visible and invisible; and in one Lord, Jesus Christ, the Son of God, Only begotten of the Father, that is to say, of the substance of the Father, God of God and Light of Light, very God of very God, begotten, not made, being of one substance with the Father, by whom all things were made, both things in heaven and things on earth; who, for us men and our salvation, came down and was made flesh, was made man, suffered, and rose again on the third day, went up into the heavens, and is to come again to judge both the quick and the dead; and in the Holy Ghost.

Unfortunately, the early stages of this discussion had failed adequately to take account of the biblical material that seemed to provide the most solid justification for identifying Jesus with the incarnate Logos: the prologue of the Fourth Gospel. Here, John had spoken eloquently of the Logos (translated as "Word" in English versions) who "became flesh, and dwelt among us" (John 1:14, NASB). Thus it seems reasonable to explore this passage as a significant source for sound Christological thinking. "*In the beginning* was the Word, and the Word was *with* God, and the Word *was* God" (v. 1). The words italicized for emphasis show the essential points in a doctrine of Christ: He is eternal; He is distinct from God; He is God. These points emphasize His divine nature.

His Deity

"In the beginning" (John 1:1) echoes the majestic words of Gen. 1:1 and is intended to convey the same sense of sovereignty in relation to the world and time. Specifically, John is affirming the *preexistence* of Christ or the Word. Although the *beginning* refers to the initial moment of the world's creation, the verb used here implies

---

3. They interpreted "begotten" as "coming into being" at a given point in time/eternity.

the *eternal* existence of the Logos as was stated of Wisdom (Old Testament counterpart of the Logos) in Prov. 8:23: "I was set up from everlasting, from the beginning, or ever the earth was." Thus the creation of which John speaks is not carried out by some subordinate being, but by the eternal Word of God.

The Fourth Gospel is noted for its double meanings, and right at the outset there seems to be one. The term "beginning" can also mean "origin" in the sense of basic cause. Bishop William Temple draws upon this twofold significance and suggests that it denotes both "in the beginning of history" and "at the root of the universe." In a parallel statement in verse 3, John explicitly spells this out: "All things were made by him; and without him was not any thing made that was made." William Barclay includes this second connotation in his interpretation and states the significance of it in the following words: "If the Word was with God before time began, if God's Word is part of the eternal scheme of things, it means that *God was always like Jesus.*"[4]

The relation of the Word to creation is that of *informing* the world with structure and meaning. It is the gospel's way of saying that we are living in a "Christian universe." The Logos did not create the world because God was too transcendent and detached to dirty His hands with such a menial task, as Arius had presupposed. Rather it was the uncreated reason of God that assures that the universe reflects the moral character of its Creator. This is the basis for what philosophers have called natural law, but natural law cannot be discussed meaningfully apart from a theological context. That is, if it is not grounded in the nature of God, it has little possibility of being established. Then "God is dead, everything is permitted," as Friedrich Nietzsche is quoted as saying. Not only does God have a moral order to which the world must conform or perish, but He has built it into the very structure of the Creation—and Jesus Christ as the Agent of Creation is the microcosm of this order.

The second phrase affirms of the Word that He was "with" God. The word "with" means "before" or "before the presence of"; or as E. F. Scott expresses it, "not absorbed in Him, but standing over against Him as a distinct person." The term safeguards the idea of His unique personality. From eternity "the Word" existed,

---

4. William Barclay, *The Gospel of John*, in *The Daily Study Bible* (Philadelphia: Westminster Press, 1955), 1:15.

literally, in a face-to-face relation to God. This is probably the most difficult concept of all for theologians to handle, especially if they are committed to a monotheistic faith. It is this point that created many of the early controversies over the person of Christ. Ancient Jews and modern Unitarians deny the Christian doctrine of the Trinity in favor of *one* God, mistaking Trinitarianism for polytheism. Actually the phrase in question indicates that the Logos existed in the closest possible connection with the Father, and it is intimacy rather than separateness that John is seeking to express. Christian theologians have always attempted to affirm reverently both one God and the reality of the Son or Logos at one and the same time, but none have ever professed to have explained it adequately. It is a mystery that transcends finite human understanding.

Although the Word existed "with" God, He was not a creature; He was the Creator of "all things" (John 1:3). It was this only Son, generated eternally[5] from the very being of the Father, who "was made flesh, and dwelt among us" as Jesus of Nazareth (v. 14).

This "becoming flesh" may be referred to in John 1:13. In some ancient manuscripts this verse has a singular verb: "Who *was* born, not of blood, nor of the will of the flesh, nor of the will of man, but of God." If this be correct,[6] John may be referring to the Virgin Birth: "The Word was made flesh" by a divine miracle, just as Luke declares (1:35). Whether or not we follow this reading does not alter the fact that the Virgin Birth was the manner by which the Eternal Son entered human history.

Many thinkers have spent their time and energy exploring the biological possibilities of the Virgin Birth. Many have even allowed an unbiblical view of sin to dictate their understanding of why the Virgin Birth was necessary. By thinking of original sin as being propagated by the sexual act,[7] they felt that sinlessness was possible only when this was absent. In distinction from these considerations the true significance of the Virgin Birth is that it points to

---

5. This term is derived from Origen, the Early Church theologian who coined the phrase "the eternal generation of the Son" to affirm His coeternality with the Father while at the same time recognizing His subordination.

6. The best manuscript evidence supports the common reading "were," although Tertullian and other church fathers accepted the variant reading.

7. This theory originated with Origen, an early Greek father, and is foreign to biblical faith. It is most commonly associated with Augustine, who was morbidly preoccupied with sin as concupiscence interpreted as sexuality.

the discontinuity of Jesus with all natural causes. As the Suffering Servant of Isaiah 53, He is "a root out of a dry ground" (v. 2). He cannot be explained as the product of any merely human precedents, but He stands as uniquely the invasion of God *into* history, rather than the product of forces *within* history.

Jesus was not another man among men, arising out of the natural processes of life. He *entered* human history; He was born *from above*. In Him eternity invaded time, God became man! The Holy Spirit overshadowing the Virgin Mary was the miracle by which this was accomplished. E. Stanley Jones always insisted that we do not believe in Jesus because of the Virgin Birth; we believe in the Virgin Birth because we believe in Jesus. He is the Son of God "who, for us men and our salvation, came down from heaven . . . and was crucified" (Nicene-Chalcedonian Creed).

The third affirmation is perhaps the most exalted claim of all for the Logos: "The Word was God." How can this be? There is virtually unanimous agreement among interpreters that John is simply saying that He was of the very essence (or being) of God the Father. "He is not saying that the Logos was identical with God; he was saying that Jesus is so perfectly the same as God in mind, in being that in Jesus we perfectly see what God is like" (Barclay). It is the sense in which Christ can be God, not the whole Godhead but a person distinct from God the Father. This poses the problem that the doctrine of the Trinity seeks to solve, as we noted above.

The Logos was not the Father, He was "the only begotten Son,[8] which is in the bosom of the Father" (John 1:18).

But even in the demonstrations of miraculous power, His deity was open only to the eyes of faith. In fact, it was primarily men of faith who were party to such manifestations. Remember, it was Peter, James, and John, the inner circle, who were with Him on the Mount of Transfiguration. Those miracles that were performed openly were recognized as such only by those who had the will to follow His teachings. It is now as it was then: Obedience to the commands and claims of Christ is the prerequisite to knowing that He is the Son of God (see John 7:17). It is in that relationship alone that we can truly recognize that in Christ the fullness of Deity dwells bodily (Col. 2:9) and that "God was in Christ, reconciling the world unto himself" (2 Cor. 5:19).

---

8. Some ancient MSS read, "the only begotten God" (μονογενής Θεός) (monogenēs theos).

His Humanity

If the liberal has difficulty retaining belief in His deity, we conservatives have equal difficulty in holding on to His humanity. This tension has been present from the earliest days of Christian thinking. Men who were known as Ebionites could confess only that Jesus was a good man, a prophet, but not "God . . . in the flesh" (1 Tim. 3:16). That was too much for their Jewish monotheism to take. Others known as Docetics[9] claimed that Jesus was fully God but that His body was merely an appearance. Their views that matter was evil would not permit them to believe in a real incarnation. Thus the Savior was but a phantom, an apparition that could fool any onlooker but was not actual flesh and bones. But both extremes were rejected by the Early Church in favor of asserting the full deity and the full humanity. He was no angel masquerading among us as a man, a seeming man; He was "bone of our bone, flesh of our flesh."

It is interesting that the book of the New Testament that exalts Jesus to the highest level of Deity at the same time lays the strongest stress upon His manhood. What greater words than those found in the prologue to Hebrews: "The Son is the radiance of God's glory and the exact representation of his being, sustaining all things by his powerful word" (1:3, NIV). Yet in 2:10 the writer notes that it was fitting that God the Father should make Christ "perfect through suffering" (NIV). In 4:15 we are reminded that "we do not have a high priest who is unable to sympathize with our weaknesses, but we have one who has been tempted in every way, just as we are" (NIV). He even "learned . . . obedience by the things which he suffered" (5:8; cf. vv. 7, 9). Hugh Ross Mackintosh summarizes it beautifully: "Nowhere in the New Testament is the humanity of Christ set forth so movingly."[10]

We have only one account of Jesus' boyhood or adolescence, and that implies that His was a completely normal development: He "grew in wisdom and stature, and in favor with God and men" (Luke 2:52, NIV). There were other stories, such as in the apocryphal Gospel of Thomas where Jesus is depicted as playing with His chums in Nazareth. They are making clay pigeons and tossing them up in the air as if in flight. Jesus' pigeons come to life and fly

---

9. From the Greek (δοκεῖν) *(dokein)*, meaning "to seem" or "appear."

10. *The Doctrine of the Person of Christ* (New York: Charles Scribner's Sons, 1915), 79.

away. It is not without reason that the Early Church excluded such accounts from the canon. They knew that Jesus was no freak, but a fully human person in every way. The humanity of Jesus is just as essential to Christian faith as His deity.

The God-man

These two dimensions of Jesus' person do not pose for us an either/or dichotomy. Rather both must be held firmly with neither one being diminished. In 2 Cor. 5:19 Paul writes, "*God* was in Christ" (italics added). Yet in 1 Timothy he writes, "There is one God, and one mediator between God and men, the man Christ Jesus; who gave himself a ransom for all" (2:5-6). Jesus was "God";[11] Jesus was a man. Not until we see both of these truths about Him do we do full justice to the New Testament witness.

We must, however, go on to recognize that while both aspects of the person of Christ are supported by the New Testament, there is no *doctrine* of the person of Christ in the New Testament. By this we mean that no attempt is made to *explain* how these two aspects are related. That Christological question was bequeathed to the theologians to work out, and it took them quite a while to do it—in fact, they are still at it. Several false starts occurred before a consensus was reached.

One ingenious explanation utilized the Greek understanding of man as a three-part being (trichotomy): body, soul, and spirit. The spirit was the rational and volitional faculty of the human person. In this theory, known as Apollinarianism (from Apollinaris who formulated it), the divine Logos assumed the role of the "spirit" in the person of Jesus so that the center of the personality of the God-man was divine. This was rejected because it deprived Jesus of *full* humanity: His was not a human spirit.

Another attempt has become known as Nestorianism (although some modern scholars are convinced that Nestorius, from whom it took its name, never taught such a doctrine). This explanation spoke of two natures within Jesus in such a way that they coexisted but did not really unite to form one person. In a sense, there were two persons. This was a violation of the formula of

---

11. We put this word in quotes to indicate that Jesus is not God *without remainder.* This excludes a view that might be called a Unitarianism of the Son prevalent among some "Jesus Only" Pentecostalist sects. This is as much a Christian heresy as historic Unitarianism of the Father.

Tertullian, whose phrase became the standard of orthodoxy: "Do not divide the Person or confuse the natures." Popular expressions of Nestorianism speak of certain acts of Jesus (such as performing miracles) as the divine part of Him at work, while other actions (such as showing grief or confessing ignorance) are ascribed to the human part. But the Christian faith insists that Jesus was one Person, not two, and so all actions were performed by one undivided Person.

The third false start violated the other warning of Tertullian not to "confuse the natures." Identified as Eutychianism (from Eutyches), it asserted that the human nature was so assimilated by the divine that its identity was lost, with the result that the Incarnation produced one divine nature. The formula was, "There were two natures before the Incarnation but only one afterward." This too was rejected by the early fathers since it resulted in the loss of Jesus' humanity.[12]

The struggle finally to formulate a doctrinal understanding of the person of Christ came to a culmination in the Chalcedonian Creed of A.D. 451:

> Following, then, the holy fathers, we unite in teaching all men to confess the one and only Son, our Lord Jesus Christ. This selfsame one is perfect both in deity and also in human-ness; this selfsame one is also actually God and actually man, with a rational soul and a body [against Apollinaris]. He is of the same reality as God as far as his deity is concerned [against Arianism] and of the same reality as we are ourselves as far as his human-ness is concerned; thus like us in all respects, sin only excepted. Before time began he was begotten of the Father, in respect of his deity, and now in these "last days," for us and on behalf of our salvation, this selfsame one was born of Mary the virgin, who is God-bearer in respect of his human-ness.
>
> [We also teach] that we apprehend this one and only Christ—Son, Lord, only-begotten—in two natures; [and we do this] without confusing the two natures, without transmuting one nature into the other [against Eutyches], without dividing them into two separate categories, without contrasting them according to area or function [against Nestorianism]. The distinctiveness of each nature is not nullified by the union. Instead, the "properties" of each nature are conserved and both natures concur in one "person" and in one *hypostasis*. They are not divided or cut into two *prosopa*, but are together the one and only and only-begotten Logos of God, the Lord Jesus Christ. Thus have the prophets of old testified; thus the Lord

---

12. The technical name for this was *monophysitism*, meaning "one nature."

Jesus Christ himself taught us; thus the Symbol of the Fathers has handed down to us.[13]

Careful scrutiny of this creed will show that its strength lies in what it rejects rather than in its positive formulations. All of the views that fell below the level of the Christian commitment to Christ were condemned as dead-end streets. It simply pins down once again the fathers' faith in Jesus' full humanity *and* deity. Perhaps we are finally driven beyond rational explanation to the acceptance of what Sören Kierkegaard called the "supreme paradox" of the Christian faith. Within the limits of our finite reason and language we cannot penetrate to the level of understanding how God and man can become so united in such an intimate union without either losing identity. Any rational explanation must ultimately have a weakness that betrays a fundamental aspect of faith. Human reason cannot fathom "the mystery of godliness: God was manifest in the flesh" (1 Tim. 3:16). But, as Browning once said, the truth of the Incarnation, accepted by reason, illumines all else!

Donald Baillie gives the helpful suggestion that the nearest we can come to explaining the Incarnation is in the paradox of grace, where we recognize in our own salvation the apparently contradictory claims that it is "I, yet not I" who is involved (see Gal. 2:20). It is all of grace, yet not without my response. Thus this paradox of Christian experience points to the even greater paradox of God becoming man in the person of Jesus Christ.[14]

The New Testament doctrine of Christ does not stop here. In one sense, all that has thus far been said is but preliminary to the gospel. The heart of the apostolic declaration is: This Jesus God offered up as the Sacrifice for the sins of the world; He was buried and descended into Hades; He was raised up from the dead and was seen of chosen witnesses; He was exalted to the Father's right hand where He received from the Father the promised Holy Spirit, whom He poured out upon the Church; He now reigns as Lord and Christ in heaven and intercedes for us there as our High Priest; He shall come again in glory to consummate our salvation and bring the victory of God's kingdom over the last enemy, death.[15]

A full-orbed doctrine of Christ must not stop with the incarnation or even the death of Christ. It must include the resurrection, ascension, intercession, and return of Christ. It was this apostolic

---

13. Taken from *Creeds of the Churches*, ed. John H. Leith (Atlanta: John Knox Press, 1977).

14. *God Was in Christ* (London: Faber and Faber, 1961).

15. Some of these themes will be explored in later chapters.

witness to Christ that constituted the *kerygma,* or saving proclamation, and which is the very core of the New Testament.[16] It is summarized in several places in the New Testament (e.g., Acts 2:22-36; Phil. 2:5-11; 1 Tim. 3:16) and in the second paragraph of the Apostles' Creed. No person can rightfully claim to be a true believer in Christ who does not receive this message. It is this apostolic proclamation that we are commanded to preach to the ends of the earth.

Suggested Additional Readings

Donald M. Baillie, *God Was in Christ,* chaps. 1—6.
Charles W. Carter, "Christ," *Beacon Dictionary of Theology,* 101-3.
Richard Longenecker, *The Christology of Early Jewish Christianity.*
H. D. McDonald, *Jesus—Human and Divine.*
James S. Stewart, *The Life and Teachings of Jesus Christ.*
Vincent Taylor, *The Person of Christ.*
J. S. Whale, *Christian Doctrine,* chap. 5.
Charles R. Wilson, "Christology," *A Contemporary Wesleyan Theology* 1:331-74.

---

16. C. H. Dodd, in *The Apostolic Preaching* (New York: Harper and Bros., 1962), has been a pioneer in isolating the central elements of the kerygma of proclamation of the Early Church.

The Holy Spirit

The Trinitarian understanding of God, which is unique to the Christian faith, arose out of the experience of the Early Church. The disciples had encountered God in Jesus Christ, and following His ascension, they experienced God as personal Presence. In David H. C. Read's words, they encountered God as always and everywhere (the Father), as there and then (the Son), and as here and now (the Spirit).[1] The Trinity was thus a spiritual reality before it was a doctrine. Unlike the average modern Christian, for whom the idea of the Holy Spirit is somewhat of a puzzlement,[2] the first Christians were keenly aware of the Holy Spirit as a present and living experience. The reason for this is that in Him Christ was alive among them and within them.

> These dispirited men and women, for whom the events of the Crucifixion and Resurrection seemed to have come and gone like a lightning flash that lit up everything for a brief moment and then died into night, were suddenly aware that God was among them, that Christ was still alive, and that what he had done was now and forever operative among them. . . . This was not a new set of ideas. It was life.[3]

---

1. In a sermon on "The National Radio Pulpit," no data available.
2. Speaking of modern man, William Barclay says, "Our thinking about the Spirit is vaguer and more undefined than our thinking about any other part of the Christian faith." *The Promise of the Spirit* (Philadelphia: Westminster Press, 1960), 11.
3. David H. C. Read, *The Christian Faith* (Nashville: Abingdon Press, 1956), 94-95.

The Trinitarian understanding of God is thus a distinctively Christian concept growing out of the experience of the Church that came to expression in the New Testament writings. They, in turn, provided the raw materials for doctrinal elaboration. However, its roots are already present in the Old Testament. In the creation account in Genesis we find, as noted earlier, an interesting use of plural words for Deity. The divine name used is *Elohim,* the plural of the generic name for God, *El.* Several plural pronouns are used, for example, "Let *us* make man in *our* image" (1:26, italics added).

How is this phenomenon to be explained? An analogy may be the most helpful. Think about these usages in comparison to an acorn. If a person who lives in a part of the world where oak trees do not grow is given an acorn, he would not know what was potentially present within that hard shell. But if he should plant it, and it germinated and grew, then when the oak tree became a reality, he would understand that the tree was potentially present all the time. It is anachronistic to talk about the Trinity in the Old Testament; but when the Christian understanding emerged, it was not in total discontinuity with the Old Testament idea of God.

What is the significance of the plural terms in the context of the Old Testament itself? They suggest that God is a *social* being and point to the fact of His *fullness* of being. He is not a lonely, solitary One who then creates out of need. He needs nothing but finds fulfillment in himself. This has great significance for the doctrine of creation, especially the creation of man in the image of God.

The *doctrine* of the Trinity was the result of a long process of development. Theologians wrestled first with the question of the full deity of the Son. When this was established by the Nicene Creed of 325, the doctrine was placed on a solid footing. It was fully established when the Council of Constantinople in 381 affirmed the full deity of the Spirit.[4]

We have already looked at the doctrine of the Father and the Son; now to complete our study of the Christian idea of God, we must consider the doctrine of the Holy Spirit. Not only has the one true and living God manifested himself historically in Jesus of Nazareth (Col. 2:9), but through Christ God gives us the Holy Spirit, by whom He truly dwells within our human persons (see John 14:23). God the Father is God *above* us; God the Son is "God *with* us"; God

---

4. Alan Richardson, *Creeds in the Making* (New York: Macmillan Co., 1969), 55-58.

the Holy Spirit is God *in* us. The one true and living God is the Triune God: Father, Son, and Holy Spirit.

> *Glory to God in Trinity,*
> *Whose names have mysteries unknown;*
> *In essence one, in Persons Three;*
> *A social nature, yet alone.*
>
> —ISAAC WATTS

The Indwelling God

The doctrine of the Holy Spirit speaks about God's relation to the world and man, or conversely man's experience of God. The full New Testament understanding of this relationship is the climax of a long history of God's seeking to actualize His presence in and among His people, beginning with Israel and climaxing with the abiding indwelling of the Holy Spirit in the Church. However one may answer the question of why it took so long for the normative understanding to emerge, the fact is that there was a process of preparation that manifested primitive characteristics at the earliest stages and became more ethical and personal in the prophets, until it reached its actualization in experience on the Day of Pentecost. Its most mature expression is found in the teaching of Paul[5] and in the Fourth Gospel. We will trace this history in broad outline.

We will be better able to understand the various stages of this development through a well-established psychological principle. All experience is informed and given shape by our own perceptions, and this is especially true of our experience of God. On the basis of this principle we can accept the fact that even though certain Old Testament people had sub-Christian experiences of God, they were truly experiences of God, though limited by their cognitive awareness. The logical conclusion of this analysis is that even today man may truly encounter God in ways that result in or

---

5. Note the significance of the words of Alasdair I. C. Heron: "In returning from the Synoptics and Acts to Paul, we find a richer conception and deeper exploration of the nature of the Spirit, of its activity, and of its inherent connection with Jesus Christ." *The Holy Spirit* (Philadelphia: Westminster Press, 1983), 44. Also, James S. Stewart: "In the primitive Christian community there was a tendency at the first—perhaps quite natural under the circumstances—to revert to the cruder conceptions of the Spirit, and to trace His working mainly in such phenomena as speaking in tongues. It was Paul who saved the nascent faith from that dangerous retrogression." *A Man in Christ* (New York: Harper and Row, Publishers, n.d.), 308.

manifest less than normative New Testament religion. This emphasizes the great importance of a sound doctrine of the Holy Spirit.

In the Old Testament the distinctive way of speaking of the Spirit is as the "Spirit of God." "Holy Spirit" is found only twice in the Old Testament, and even these references are not to be taken in the sense commonly intended by Christian usage. Furthermore, the Spirit's relation to men is characteristically described as "coming upon" them. It was also usually temporary in nature.

"Coming upon" is particularly appropriate to speak of the way in which men experienced the Spirit of God under the old covenant. The Hebrew word translated Spirit is *Ruach* and also means "breath" or "wind," particularly a desert wind that rushes through the cedars and roars down the wadis. In like fashion the Spirit seizes men, invades them, and shakes them, giving them power to do mighty deeds or say perceptive words.

One notable feature of this experience in many of its earliest expressions is that it does not necessarily include an ethical element. Subjects like Samson leave much to be desired. Even in some instances those seized by the Spirit manifest behavior not altogether socially acceptable. After Saul was anointed to be king of Israel, he joined a band of ecstatic prophets and, stimulated by music, was seized by the Spirit. This gave rise to the rather surprised saying, "Is Saul also among the prophets?" It was not particularly a compliment (1 Sam. 10:6; 19:23-24).

The persons who were most notable subjects of Spirit seizure were the *judges,* men and women who were raised up as charismatic leaders to save the people from their enemies when they had repented of their sins. The empowerment that came upon these people enabled them to do extraordinary military and physical feats and successfully challenge the people to rally to the cause. The larger population apparently never experienced this exhilarating encounter.

Early in Israel's history, though, there appeared a desire that all of God's people be recipients of the Spirit. Moses, an exception to the general pattern of temporary Spirit endowment for leadership, gave voice to this hope in a statement that reflected a magnanimous spirit: "Would that all the Lord's people were prophets, that the Lord would put his spirit upon them!" (Num. 11:29, RSV). He unselfishly desired that the Spirit of charismatic leadership resting upon him should be more widely distributed. Later prophets gave more precise expression to this as they described the contours of the Day of the Lord that should come. Joel's picture of this great day included the expectation of an outpouring of the Spirit upon "all flesh," giving endowment to prophesy (Joel 2:28 ff.). This hope has sometimes been referred to as the *democratization* of the Spirit.

Thus there arose among Israel's expectations the hope that the age to come would be an age of the Spirit, which should be somehow connected with the Messiah. When Jesus launched His ministry in Nazareth, He did so by announcing that the words of Isa. 61:1-2 were fulfilled: "The Spirit of the Lord is on me, because he has anointed me to preach good news to the poor. He has sent me to proclaim freedom for the prisoners and recovery of sight for the blind, to release the oppressed, to proclaim the year of the Lord's favor" (Luke 4:18-21, NIV).

Jesus thus embodied the new relationship and became the pattern of the Spirit-filled life that would become available to His disciples upon the completion of His work. In John 14—16, Jesus speaks of the coming age of the Spirit and the culmination of His own ministry in terms of the Comforter—the indwelling of God within His followers (see John 14:23).

Here we must examine one of the most crucial truths to be found in the New Testament: *Christ's glorification is the absolute condition of the Gift of the Spirit.* Jesus announced at the Feast of Tabernacles, "If any one thirst, let him come to me and drink. He who believes in me, as the scripture has said, 'Out of his heart shall flow rivers of living water.'" John quickly adds a parenthetic statement of explanation: "Now this he said about the Spirit, which those who believed in him were to receive; for as yet the Spirit had not been given, because Jesus was not yet glorified" (John 7:37-39, RSV).

"Glorified" is the distinctive Johannine word for the passion, resurrection, and ascension of Jesus. While the Synoptics (Matthew, Mark, and Luke) do not speak explicitly of this, it is implied in the fact that they never have a word concerning the Gift of the Spirit on the lips of the preresurrected Jesus.

The new relationship that was to be soon inaugurated could only come to pass after Jesus had completed His mission. What is the significance of this? The answer to this question brings us to the heart of the New Testament understanding of the Holy Spirit. God indwelling His people in a "permanent" rather than a "passing" relation is somehow closely related to the completion of Jesus' mission, and *the most obvious answer is that this new reality must be the result of a new understanding of the Spirit.*

It is quite clear that this new coming of the Spirit was to bring power, and this power was to be instrumental in bringing in the Kingdom. It made all the difference in the world how this power was conceived and what the nature of the Kingdom was. If this great power had been given to the disciples *before* Jesus' ascension, they would have still been enamored of the idea of a political kingdom restored to Israel. Furthermore, this power would have been exercised in ways much like the Old Testament judges, for they had been nurtured in the idea that Messianic power would be manifested in overwhelming display that would compel acceptance.

But Jesus' passion, resurrection, and ascension demonstrated that the ultimate power was the power of suffering; that in the Cross He overcame every enemy by submission. *This would let the disciples know that the power of the Spirit that was to work through them to establish the Kingdom was the power of servanthood, of suffering love.*

It was, in a word, necessary for them to know that the Holy Spirit was the Spirit of Christ. In fact, those two designations may be used interchangeably (see Rom. 8:9-11; Eph. 3:16-19). It is this that E. Stanley Jones had in mind when he stated: "The Holy Spirit is a distinctly Christian conception. The Spirit of God is the Old Testament word. The Holy Spirit is the New Testament word. The content of Jesus has gone into it."[6] God indwelling His people is an *in-Christ-ment.* Thus the character being produced in them by this indwelling is Christlikeness. All this was implicit in the Spirit's outpouring on the Day of Pentecost and is given full elaboration in the teaching of Paul.

There is another dimension of God's relating himself to His people, and that is embodied in the word "among." This too finds its roots in the Old Testament but finds its full realization in the New Testament Church.

God dwelt with Israel in the cloud of glory that first appeared when they were in the process of becoming a people at the Exodus. In fact, it might be said with justification that it was this Presence

---

6. *The Way to Power and Poise* (Nashville: Abingdon-Cokesbury Press, 1949), 47.

around which the people clustered that constituted them a united nation. This Presence became more formalized in relation to the Tabernacle when the cloud of glory suspended itself over the Holiest of All and later in the Temple.

It was the realization of the importance of the Divine Presence that gave such prestige to the Temple in Israel's later life. The Temple was conceived as the place where God was uniquely to be found. The visions of Ezekiel are illuminating here. In an intriguing series of vignettes the clairvoyant prophet sees the glory of God reluctantly withdraw by degrees from the Temple (Ezekiel 10). With its final departure the raison d'être for Israel has ceased to be, and the end is inevitable. But when Ezekiel sees the golden age in the future, one of its central aspects is the return of the glory to the restored Temple (43:1-4).

All of this undergoes a transformation in New Testament theology. *The Temple becomes the Church of the Living God, and the Holy Spirit indwelling each individual believer constitutes him a part of the "new people."* This is why the Day of Pentecost is properly interpreted as the birthday of the Church. Just as the guiding Presence called the old Israel into being, so the Holy Spirit calls the new Israel into being.

Stephen was the first to give explicit expression to this great truth when he declared in his defense of the new faith that God "dwelleth not in temples made with hands" (Acts 7:48-50). The Jews who heard him correctly knew that he was saying that God was through with the Temple. The Church is the habitation of the Spirit, and it is as the members in particular are bound together in a real community that God is among His people. "Where two or three have gathered together in My name, there I am in their midst" (Matt. 18:20, NASB).

Paul explicitly states this new reality when he says *of the Church* in 1 Cor. 3:16: "Do you not know that you are a temple of God, and that the Spirit of God dwells in you?" (NASB) and fully spells out the imagery of the new temple in Eph. 2:19-22.

The Active God

To speak about the Holy Spirit is also to speak about *God in action.* David H. C. Read calls attention to the kinds of words that are associated in the New Testament with the Holy Spirit: " 'life,' 'love,' 'power,' 'unity,' 'fellowship'—all having reference to the practical effects of the presence of God in our human life," and comments, "To believe in the Spirit means therefore that God for us can never be a mere idea, or a distant Deity without interest in his world."[7]

The activity of God as Spirit may be discussed in three ways:[8]

(1) By God's Spirit we are *maintained in life* from moment to moment. The Nicene Creed affirms this in these words: "I believe in the Holy Spirit, the Lord and Giver of life." As noted, the word rendered "Spirit" in the Old Testament is the same as breath. As Gen. 2:7 says, it was the breath or Spirit of God breathed into man's nostrils that transformed him from a "lump of clay" into a "living being" (RSV). Thus man's life is the result of the life-force that is the Spirit of God, and when this Spirit is withdrawn, man returns to the dust (Eccles. 12:7; Ps. 146:4).

In the strange story of Gen. 6:1-8 designed to highlight the great depravity of the human race, God sets a boundary to man's life span by decreeing that His "spirit shall not abide in man for ever" (v. 3, RSV). In order to limit the continual perpetuity of his wickedness, man's life is set at no more than 120 years.

A similar use but with more spiritual overtones is found in Ezek. 37:1-14, where the army of corpses resulting from the re-gathering of the scattered bones of human skeletons is given vitality by the Spirit. This is a reconstituted Israel, given new life out of the boneyard of Babylonian captivity, and it involves more than mere life.

Of far greater theological significance is the second way of speaking of God in action as Spirit: (2) By God's Spirit we find the *new life in Christ*. It is the Spirit who awakens us from our spiritual sleep and upon our response gives us the new birth to eternal life.

In His discourses in the Upper Room, Jesus talks about the coming of the Holy Spirit and His function when He is sent. "When he comes, he will convince the world concerning sin and righteousness and judgment" (John 16:8, RSV). And in His conversation with Nicodemus He speaks of the Spirit as the vehicle of the new birth; in fact, He equates being "born from above" (marg.: KJV, NASB, NIV, RSV) with being "born of the Spirit" (3:1-8).

Every flicker of spiritual interest, every longing for holiness, every move toward God must be attributed to the activity of the Spirit. There is no initiative on our part except it is activated by the

---

7. *The Christian Faith*, 96.
8. Read suggests but does not develop this outline.

Spirit of God. His work as the sole source of Christian life is high-lighted by Paul in connection with the central New Testament confession when he writes, "No one can say 'Jesus is Lord' except by the Holy Spirit" (1 Cor. 12:3, RSV).

Having responded to the initial work of the Spirit, we are ready to experience the third point. (3) By God's Spirit we are guided forward in the Christian life and led into new reaches of truth and love. He is thus the *sanctifying* Spirit (Rom. 15:16; 2 Thess. 2:13).

In 2 Cor. 3:18 we find the normal movement of the Christian life as perfectly embodied as in any passage in the New Testament: "And we all, with unveiled face, beholding the glory of the Lord [in the face of Jesus Christ], are being changed into his likeness from one degree of glory to another; for this comes from the Lord who is the Spirit" (RSV). This increasing conformity to the likeness of Christ, which is the truly dynamic aspect of holiness, is energized and directed by the Holy Spirit. In fact the Spirit and the Lord Jesus are so closely related in this process that the apostle seems to equate the two (see 1 Cor. 15:45).[9]

Charles Wesley captures this aspect of the Spirit in these words:

> *Author of every work divine,*
> *Who dost through both creations shine.*
> *The God of nature and of grace.*
> *Thou art the Universal Soul,*
> *The plastic power that fills the whole,*
> *And governs earth, air, sea, and sky;*
> *The creatures all Thy breath receive,*
> *And who by Thy inspiring live,*
> *Without Thy inspiration die.*
>
> *Spirit immense, eternal Mind,*
> *Thou on the souls of lost mankind*
> *Dost Thy benignest influence move,*
> *Pleased to restore the ruined race,*
> *And recreate the world of grace*
> *In all the image of Thy love.*

---

9. See Eph. 2:18, however, where Paul distinguishes the Spirit from Jesus.

The living God—the Father and the Spirit—were present Jesus Christ. Likewise, the Father and the Son are present in the Holy Spirit. To be indwelt by the Holy Spirit is to be filled with all the fullness of God. Jesus Christ is God *with* us; the Holy Spirit is God *in* us. To know this is to know the love of God that transcends human knowledge! (Cf. Eph. 3:19.)

Suggested Additional Reading

Milton S. Agnew, "Pneumatology," *A Contemporary Wesleyan Theology* 1:415-72.

Arnold E. Airhart, "Holy Spirit," *Beacon Dictionary of Theology,* 262-64.

Myron S. Augsburger, *Practicing the Presence of the Spirit.*

William Barclay, *The Promise of the Spirit.*

George B. Duncan, *The Person and Work of the Holy Spirit in the Life of the Believer.*

W. M. Greathouse, *The Fullness of the Spirit.*

Michael Green, *I Believe in the Holy Spirit.*

The Spirit and the New Age, ed. Alex R. G. Deasley and R. Larry Shelton, vol. 5 of *Wesleyan Theological Perspectives.*

PART II

Man, Sin, and Grace

The Nature of Man

Classical Christian theology has consistently stated that knowledge of God and man are the twin objects of doctrinal study. It has also insisted that God is known only as He is in relation to man, which means that He cannot be known as He is in himself. Conversely man is only known fully in his relation to God. Other disciplines may explore his nature in relation to the rest of the created order, but it is the unique task of theology to identify his nature in relation to the Creator. We have looked at some facets of the nature of God in Part I of this book, and now we turn to the second, the nature of man, along with some related doctrines.

"What is man?" is a question that human thinkers have been exploring for centuries. Man is his own biggest problem, and that fact largely arises out of his inability to grasp who he is. Many attempts have been made to define human reality, some serious, some ludicrous.

The familiar story of Diogenes, the Greek teacher of philosophy, bears repeating. He suggested to his students that man may be defined as a "featherless biped." Undaunted and disbelieving, one of his pupils returned to class the next day and laid before his instructor a plucked chicken with the remark, "Behold: philosophic man!" Mark Twain is reputed to have defined man as a "laughing animal," but one tends to think of the hyena. In a more serious vein, early Greek philosophers quite naturally identified the essence of man with his rational capacity and came up with the standard definition: "Man is a rational animal." The problem with this from a theological perspective is chiefly that it seeks to define man in terms of his difference from other aspects of creation—from below rather than from above. But, as noted above, that is the best philosophy can do if it is limited to empirical knowledge.

Man can never be adequately understood in his nature, his predicament, or his destiny unless he is understood as a creature of God. Anthropology, as such, is thus not really an appropriate part of theological study except for illustrative purposes. Its methodology limits it to describing man in relation to the rest of the natural order. By contrast, the Christian view of man is through and through theological; that is, man is analyzed from above. In this light, Christian doctrine requires that man be viewed in three ways: (1) as a person created in the image of God, (2) as a sinner alienated from God and therefore corrupt and depraved in nature, and (3) as the recipient of God's redeeming grace through Christ.

Created in the Divine Image

Christian thinking about man has been influenced by two streams of thought: Hellenistic (Greek philosophy) and Hebraic (Old Testament). Many theologians have followed Hellenistic ideas without realizing that in doing so, they are interpreting human nature from a point of view foreign to divine revelation. As noted above, Hellenism has stressed the rational function of man, and those whose thinking is informed by this tradition have attempted to define the image of God in terms of man's rationality.

There are several problems that ensue when this interpretation is followed through to its logical conclusions. First, man's predicament is seen to be lack of understanding; sin is defined as ignorance. In accordance with this, salvation becomes a process of education, letting man know what he needs to do. Both points fall far short of the seriousness of biblical faith.

The Hebraic view, by contrast, understands the *Imago Dei* as a distinctly theological concept. This means that it is not a natural capacity but a relationship within which man stands. It is more appropriate to speak of man as created in the image of God than of the image of God in man. Although it is a very subtle difference, the latter way of putting it suggests that the image is something

within man, whereas the former suggests the relational understanding, which is more biblical.

But the Bible presents us with an ambiguous picture concerning this relationship. In the Old Testament, the assumption is made
that even after the Fall, man is still in the image of God (Gen. 9:6).
The New Testament, on the other hand, speaks of salvation as
restoring man to the image of God, assuming that the relation has
been broken. Are we faced with a contradiction? These facts, says
Emil Brunner, highlight the necessity of theology, for it is precisely
this discipline that takes the raw material from biblical exegesis
and integrates it into a systematic whole. The two *apparently* di-
vergent teachings are actually pointing to a fundamental truth
about man with which theology has historically attempted to come
to terms, but often in quite inadequate ways. The most common
way of trying to explain this has been to distinguish between the
moral image and the *natural* image. The former was lost in the Fall,
while the latter was retained. There are several problems with this
distinction, not the least of which is that to use the term *natural
image* is to express a contradiction in terms. If it is the image of
God, it is not natural.

By far the better way is to speak of both in terms of a relationship, referring to the broken relationship as man's *existential*
condition and the unbroken relationship as his *essential* condition.
Thus man is "essentially good but existentially estranged."[1] Classical Christian theology stands solidly behind this claim with but
few dissenting voices. From the Christian point of view, it is this
essential relation that constitutes man as man and distinguishes
him from all other creatures. The *Imago Dei* is a relationship that is
both broken *and* retained.

Of all earthly creatures only human beings are, in John Wesley's phrase, "capable of God." It is this capacity for God that is the
distinctive mark of man in the divine image. Man stands in a
unique relationship to his Creator. He may obey God and enjoy
holy communion with his Heavenly Father, or he may disobey and
discover the judgment and wrath of God. But escape God he cannot, even in hell (Ps. 139:8).

---

1. Paul Tillich, *Systematic Theology*, 3 vols. (Chicago: University of Chicago Press,
1967), 1:61 ff. Donald Bloesch, *Essentials of Evangelical Theology*, 2 vols. (San Francisco:
Harper and Row, 1978), 1:95; T. A. Kantonen, *The Theology of Evangelism* (Philadelphia:
Muhlenberg Press, 1954), 37.

The *essential* image of God, therefore, is man's responsible personhood. Like his Creator, man is personal. As a person man was made for God: "Thou hast made us for thyself, and our souls are restless till they rest in Thee" (Augustine). Nothing we may ever do can change that. Sin may mar, but it cannot destroy the essential *Imago*. Man does not become an animal by descending to bestial conduct. Nor does he become a god when he says with Sartre, "The chief project of man is to become God." Man is a creature of God, standing in an immutable relation to his Creator. "The chief end of man is to glorify God and enjoy Him forever" (Westminster Catechism), Sartre notwithstanding. Nothing can ever change that. In his *esse*, his true being, man is a person created to find his fulfillment in God. There is a "God-shaped vacuum" in the heart of every human being, as Billy Graham insists.

The *existential* image of God is constituted by a right relation to God. As originally created, man was in right relation to God and lived a life of unbroken communion and filial obedience. But this divine-human relation involved three other relations also: a right relation to other persons embodied in the male-female factor, a right relation to the earth as man exercised his God-appointed dominion over the rest of creation, and a right relation to himself as he submitted to the sovereignty of his Creator and recognized his own creaturely status.

All these relations constituted *primitive holiness,* which was derived from God and not inherent in Adam. Human holiness is always relational and derivative. Only God is essentially holy. Many have attempted to depict this relation of dependency with the analogy of a mirror. As a mirror reflects the image of one's face when in proper position before it, so Adam reflected the holy love of God and imaged his Creator. Indwelt by the Spirit, man was the temple of God and therefore holy in nature. Likewise, *we are holy only as we are rightly related to God and truly indwelt by His sanctifying Spirit.* Our essential nature is nonforfeitable; our existential image has been destroyed by sin and can only be restored when we return to right relation to God.

Fallen from God

The most obvious fact about the human predicament is that man has fallen away from his original right relation to God. This fallenness is the point of the traditional doctrine of *original sin.* "Explain original sin any way you choose," Edward T. Ramsdell once said in a university lecture, "you cannot explain it away—it is an empirical fact." *Essentially* man is good, a person made for God. *Existentially* he is sinful, a rebel alienated from the life of God and therefore corrupt. Man is a Rolls-Royce—totaled!

In the Epistle of Romans we have three pictures of fallen man. In 1:18-32 Paul gives the *theological* meaning of original sin. Although created by God, man refused to acknowledge the sovereignty of his Creator. This rebellion is an unbroken characteristic of the human race. It is not the consequence of ignorance but the deliberate rejection of a universal knowledge made available to all persons by the Creator. They have willfully chosen to worship the creature rather than the Creator. Therefore, man's foolish heart is darkened, and his entire existence is distorted and corrupted by evil.

This analysis provides us with the clue to the essence of sinfulness. In the film *Jesus of Nazareth,* when Herod the Great learns from the wise men that a king has been born, he utters these classic words: "This is my world; I will not share it with another. There is no room for two kings here." No better illustration of the essence of sin portrayed by the apostle could be found.

In Rom. 5:12-21 Paul gives the *historical* meaning of original sin. Through Adam's disobedience sin entered the human race and death by sin. In this passage Adam and Christ are more than two individuals; they embody the old humanity and the new humanity—the old humanity dead in sin and the new humanity alive to God and free from sin.

Another way of viewing this is to see Adam and Christ as representing two spheres or realms of existence, commonly referred to in New Testament idiom as the "present age" and the "age to come."

> In speaking of the two ages, however, we must avoid thinking simply in terms of datable events in history. In one sense the new age may be said to have begun with the death and resurrection of Jesus (*ca.* A.D. 30). Yet in another sense we are positing *two overlapping orders of existence.* Every person is either in Adam (by birth) or in Christ (by faith). God's justifying act removes us from the old Adamic order and places us in "the new creation" (the new race) of which Christ is the Head. In thus writing of Adam and Christ, Paul does not think of humanity as a chance gathering of individuals but as an organic

unity, a single body under a single head. That head is either Christ or Adam.[2]

Paul makes no attempt to explain how it occurs but simply proclaims the fact that by birth we are all in Adam. We were born into a *race* that has been alienated from the life of God and is therefore dead in sin. Our human inheritance is that of sin and death. But "A Second Adam to the fight / And to the rescue came!" Adam's disobedience was an act of *human perfidy*, resulting in death and sin; Christ's obedience was an act of *divine grace*, making possible life and holiness (vv. 15, 19-21). *By faith we are incorporated into the risen Christ and inherit the abounding grace that has expelled sin!* Our natural inheritance from Adam is death and sin; our spiritual inheritance from Christ is life and holiness!

In Rom. 7:14-25 Paul gives the *existential* meaning of original sin, the personal and inward struggle that ensues from human fallenness. As fallen creatures we are "carnal, sold under sin" (v. 14). "I know that in me (that is, in my flesh,) dwelleth no good thing: for to will is present with me; but how to perform that which is good I find not" (v. 18). By "flesh" here, Wesley explains, Paul means "the whole man as he is by nature." By nature I am "flesh." While the apostle uses "flesh" to refer to meat and bones and sometimes to indicate the frailty of finitude, his most distinctive use is in a religious sense, as here. It does not refer to the matter of man's body or even a part of his whole being but to a *self-centered* existence. The "flesh" is "I" living for myself, the perverted bent of the whole person. Jesus declared, "That which is born of the flesh is flesh" (John 3:6)—and therefore in need of rebirth from above.

Not only is it true that flesh cannot please God, but man apart from grace has no true freedom; he is free only to sin. When he would do good, evil is present. His will may choose, but it cannot perform the good. He may desperately struggle to do God's will, but ultimately he is reduced to sheer despair. He cries, "O wretched man that I am! who shall deliver me from the body of this death?" (Rom. 7:24).

Romans 7 proves that the law can no more sanctify than it can justify. Under the law man hears God's demands but is powerless to love and obey God. This is Paul's whole point in this chapter. He summarizes his argument in the last sentence: "So then with the

---

2. W. M. Greathouse, "Romans," in *Beacon Bible Commentary*, 10 vols. (Kansas City: Beacon Hill Press of Kansas City, 1968), 8:113-14.

mind I myself serve the law of God; but with the flesh [I left to myself, I depending on myself] the law of sin" (7:25). Left to myself I am *flesh,* and therefore impotent of good.

The Twofold Nature of Sin

Sin is a rebellion. John Wesley's classic definition of sin as a "wilful transgression of a known law of God" is often quoted but widely misunderstood. At first blush one gets the impression that sin is a legalistic matter, the simple fact of breaking a law. It is because Wesley's critics mistake him to be saying this that they criticize him for not taking sin seriously.

But Wesley was a much better theologian than that. This definition really points to the attitude that underlies any lawbreaking, an attitude of rebelliousness, or as 1 John 3:4 puts it when properly translated: "sin is lawlessness" (NASB, NIV, RSV, cf. NEB).

From the biblical perspective, this "lawlessness" roots in man's refusal to accept his role as creature (created being) with the consequent attempt to become his own god. In a word it is self-sovereignty. If we look at the Genesis story of the temptation and fall of man, this will become clear. The serpent suggests to Eve that if she will eat of the forbidden fruit, she will become "as god" (cf. 3:5). And after she and Adam did so, God passed the judgment on the pair: They have "become as one of us" (v. 22).

The essence of sin then is a "revolt against heaven." It is throwing over the divine Lordship and assuming the reins of one's own life. Isa. 53:6 pinpoints it accurately when it says: "All we like sheep have gone astray; *we have turned every one to his own way*" (italics added). This is far more profound than breaking a law, even a divine law; it is a matter of ownership, of Lordship, of who is sovereign in my life.

Sin is an enslavement. Sin is far more than a free choice to do "one's own thing"; it is a condition in which man finds himself unable to do otherwise. The superficial view of sin that sees salvation to be a mere human decision to change "owners," to stop breaking God's laws and begin keeping them, is associated with a British monk by the name of Pelagius and is known as Pelagianism.

For Pelagius, every person is born in the same condition as Adam, a sort of spiritual tabula rasa with the native capacity to decide to be a Christian. God offers him the teaching of the Scriptures and the example of Christ, and it is his decision whether to follow these. The universality of sin is explained as the effects of the unbroken bad example of the human race.

By contrast, Augustine, following Paul, insisted that man as a fallen being is free only to sin. No amount of good intention or self-exertion can result in salvation. In a word, man finds himself shackled hand and foot; his will is enslaved. Therefore there is need for a liberation, a deliverance, a healing so that man can be given a "gracious ability" to turn to his Maker.

A Concluding Distinction

The preceding analysis of the human predicament recognizes the twofold nature of sin (original and actual) and implies that a genuine gospel (good news) will provide a twofold remedy (justification and sanctification). In the chapter that follows we shall consider in detail this twofold provision as we explore the concept of the Atonement. But at this point we will take a closer look at the human predicament. This will entail an endeavor to understand more fully the difference between original and actual sin, or the state of sinfulness and the acts of sin.

Sin in human existence is fundamentally a *state* of self-centeredness resulting from man's turning from God as his chief end. In his "Doctrine of Original Sin" Wesley observes:

> Man was created looking directly to God, as his last end; but, falling into sin, he fell off from God, and turned into himself. Now, this infers [sic] a total apostasy and universal corruption in man; for where the last end is changed, there can be no real goodness. And this is the case of all men in their natural state: They seek not God, but themselves. Hence though many fair shreds of morality are among them, yet "there is none that doeth good, no, not one." For though some of them "run well," they are still off the way; they never aim at the right mark. Whithersoever they move, they cannot move beyond the circle of self. They seek themselves, they act for themselves; their natural, civil, and religious actions, from whatever spring they come, do all run into, and meet in, this dead sea.[3]

Wesley variously termed original sin to be atheism, unbelief, pride, or idolatry. "Call it what you will," he said, the concept, not the term, is what matters. Man's predicament is, as Luther put it,

---

3. *The Works of John Wesley*, 3rd ed. (Kansas City: Beacon Hill Press of Kansas City, 1978), 9:456.

that his heart is turned in on itself *(cor incurvatum in se)*. As a result of his turning from God, he is caught in a vicious circle of idolatry and inevitably turns for satisfaction to himself or things.

This state of self-idolatry and depravity is native to our human situation as members of a fallen race: "That which is born of the flesh is flesh" (John 3:6). Deprived of the Spirit's sanctifying control as members of Adam's fallen race, we inevitably fall into the sin of self-sovereignty. Echoing Paul's statement in Eph. 2:3, Nels Ferré writes, "We, by nature, turn self-affirmation into a denial of the supremacy of God and of the prior demand of fellowship. We, by nature, rebel against God and His purpose for our lives."[4]

This state of sin, however, must be distinguished from the act of sin. The latter involves, as the former does not, personal guilt incurred by conscious, willful disobedience. Admittedly, it is difficult if not impossible to pinpoint the moment in our personal history when original sin becomes actual sin. Nevertheless, Paul speaks for us all when he confesses, "I was once alive apart from the law, but when the commandment came [home to the conscience], sin revived and I died" (Rom. 7:9, RSV). At the very threshold of moral responsibility every individual personally rebels against the truth of God and experiences divine condemnation. It is this willful self-separation from God that is properly denominated actual sin.[5]

The distinction between original and actual sin is fundamental to the further differentiation between justification and sanctification, as Grensted shows:

> *Sin* is a disposition directed toward a wrong object, wrongness being determined at each level, by the refusal to turn to God or to His symbolic surrogate. *Sins* are acts proceeding from such a disposition, and are therefore secondary and symptomatic. We may make the distinction clear by saying that sins need *forgiveness,* while sin needs *cure.*[6]

---

4. *The Christian Faith* (New York and London: Harper and Bros., 1942), 115.

5. For Paul, it is the law understood as divine commandment that turns sin into transgression (Rom. 4:15; 5:20; 7:7-13). Cf. *Beacon Bible Commentary* (Kansas City: Beacon Hill Press of Kansas City, 1968), 8:103-4, 122-24, 148-53.

6. Ferré, *Christian Faith,* 187 n.

Recipient of God's Grace

To stop with the above point is to leave the human race in a helpless, hopeless plight. Paul's final word was not a word of despair but a word of hope: "I thank God through Jesus Christ our Lord" (Rom. 7:25).

The whole meaning of redemption is that God has *not* left humankind to save themselves. Through Christ He has potentially redeemed the entire race! If "by one man sin entered into the world, and death by sin . . . even so by the righteousness of one the free gift came upon all men unto justification of life" (Rom. 5:12, 18). The "free gift" is the gift of God's prevenient grace. This grace is "free *for* all and free *in* all" (Wesley). While it is true that if we are left to ourselves there is no hope of our salvation, God has not left us to ourselves. The Spirit of God is at work in every sinner's heart, seeking to awaken, convict, convert, and sanctify him. This is what we mean by "prevenient" grace: God comes to every one of us by the Holy Spirit and gently strives to save us from ourselves.

God's prevenient grace frees our will sufficiently to enable us to call on Christ and be delivered. Through the *forgiving* grace of God we may be *justified*—pardoned from sin and accepted of God as though we had never sinned. Through the *transforming* grace of God we may be *sanctified*—set free from sin's dominion (in the new birth) and being (in entire sanctification) and restored to the moral likeness of God (in the total process), by the power of the transforming Spirit. Through God's resurrection grace we shall ultimately be *glorified*—resurrected with Christ when He returns, and transformed into His complete likeness, to enjoy His glory forever![7]

Suggested Additional Reading

Ray S. Anderson, *On Becoming Human.*
David Cairns, *The Image of God in Man.*
Charles W. Carter, "Anthropology," *A Contemporary Wesleyan Theology* 1:195-236.
John Macmurray, *Persons in Relation.*
Marianne Micks, *Our Search for Identity.*
Eric Sauer, *King of the Earth.*
J. S. Whale, *Christian Doctrine,* chap. 2.

---

7. These various designations of "kinds" of grace are not intended to make scholastic distinctions as if "grace" were something other than the activity of God himself with some sort of qualitative distinction among them. God does not have several "grace bins" in which He keeps a separate store of each kind. This is simply the theological way of speaking about the multifaceted mercy of God.

The Atonement

In the previous chapter we anticipated the topic under discussion here. We saw that man the sinner is the object of God's grace in Christ. Because God made man for himself and loves him, He cannot leave man in his sin and despair. How God works to bring man out of his predicament is known theologically as the doctrine of the Atonement.

There have been a number of theories of the Atonement advanced during the history of Christian thought, some of which stand nearer to the heart of the New Testament message than others. The New Testament itself offers several suggestive images of the work of Christ, none of which was developed into a full-orbed theory by the biblical writers. Theologians have picked up on some of these images and used them to work out particular understandings of the Atonement. Theologians today generally recognize that, while most of these theories reflect a basic truth, no one by itself provides us with the final answer to the question of how the death of Christ effected a reconciliation between man and God.

Each of these theories is a theological construction that expresses a particular understanding of the nature of God, the nature of sin, and the nature of the divine-human relation and is also informed by a particular cultural experience.

Using these reference points, we will do a cursory survey of the classical Atonement theories and point out the Wesleyan position on the points mentioned above so as to be able to suggest a view consistent with Wesleyan theology.

Classical Views

The Ransom Theory. This interpretation builds upon the words of Jesus in Matt. 20:28: "Even as the Son of man came not to be ministered unto, but to minister, and to give his life a ransom for many." It elaborates this metaphor into a fully articulated picture of the human predicament and the divine solution. Man, in Adam, has sold himself into slavery to the devil. Being unable to redeem (buy back) himself, there must be someone able and willing to pay a ransom price demanded by the captor. God entered into an agreement with the devil and gives His Son as the ransom in His death to set man free. The catch is that while man was liberated from his bondage, Satan also lost his prize, since God raised Jesus from the dead and reclaimed Him from the enemy's clutches. It is easy enough to see that here sin is viewed as slavery and God as the Deliverer who in love pays the price to set men free. Such a construction spoke meaningfully to persons in an ethos that fostered a sense of human helplessness.

Gustav Aulen, a Swedish bishop, has attempted to reinstate a modern version of this theory, free of the curious twists given to it by some of the early fathers, referring to it as the "classical view" of the Atonement, since it was the prevalent understanding of Christ's work for the first 1,000 years of Christian history. He has referred to it by the term *Christus Victor* (Christ the Victor) to highlight the triumph of Jesus over the enemy to set men free. Thus the Atonement provides the way of ransoming man from the bondage of sin in which he is enmeshed.

The Satisfaction Theory. This view, advocated by Anselm (1033-1109), replaced the ransom theory as the dominant one in the Western church. It arose in the context of feudal society, and its basic categories are shaped by that cultural milieu. God is conceived as a feudal lord, and man is the serf whose responsibility is to render the Lord his appropriate respect. Sin is an outrage to the honor of God that must be satisfied before the serf can be restored to divine favor. Since humankind is finite in nature and incapable of rendering the proper satisfaction, God sent His Son to become the God-man (Anselm's central work was titled *Cur Deus Homo* [Why the God-man]) in order to render satisfaction to God. The cultural conditioning of this view is more obvious than in most others.

The Penal Satisfaction Theory. Building upon the new interest in law arising out of the Renaissance, John Calvin developed a different form of the satisfaction theory. God was conceived as the Sovereign Lawgiver and sin as the violation of the law. Since any violation of law must be punished, and satisfaction rendered to the divine justice before forgiveness and restoration, the death of Jesus (as a man) was His bearing the punishment justly due to man the sinner. This rational balancing of justice and mercy made the divine-human relation a legal transaction and subject to the demands of impersonal justice. The logical consequence of it was that if a substitute was punished for the violation of the law, the actual lawbreaker could go free and did not need to face the consequence of his sin. The law was satisfied, but the sinner remained a sinner. Furthermore, if the law was satisfied by Christ's death, those for whom He died (was punished) were thereby saved, since the law was satisfied and there was no need for further punishment. Either Jesus died for all men, resulting in universalism, or for only some, resulting in particular election. Calvin chose the latter option, since it was obvious that all men were not saved.

The Moral Influence Theory. The name of Abelard is traditionally associated with this view, which is a reaction against the impersonal character and legalism of the satisfaction theories. Its emphasis is upon the love of God, and it views the divine-human relation in personal terms. The death of Christ serves as an example of God's love, which offers free and full forgiveness. Its greatest weakness consists in its failure to take with full seriousness the binding power of sin.

Wesleyan Presuppositions

In brief, the Wesleyan view of God emphasizes His nature as *holy love.* As Wesley says in his note on 1 John 4:8—"God is often styled holy, righteous, wise; but not holiness, righteousness, or wisdom in the abstract, as He is said to be love: intimating that this is His darling, His reigning attribute, the attribute that sheds an amiable glory on all His other perfections." This understanding precludes the possibility of a limited Atonement such as the penal satisfaction theory entails. Since love is an expression of God's nature, it is universal in its scope, resulting in a view of universal Atonement. It is not that all men *will* be saved, but that all men *may* be saved since Jesus died for all.

Sin, in the Wesleyan context, is seen as personal in nature rather than legal. While it may entail the disobedience of laws, the root of such disobedience is a rebellious spirit that erects a barrier to fellowship with God. Although God's universal love reaches out to all men, His holiness cannot establish fellowship in the situation of sin. Hence the death of Christ is directed toward the removal of the sin that stands as a barrier to reconciliation. In fact, the fundamental meaning of the term translated as atonement *is* reconciliation.

In the light of this, Wesleyan theology is committed to the belief that the Atonement provides for a full remedy of the sin problem:

> *My sin—oh, the bliss of this glorious thought!—*
> *My sin—not in part, but the whole—*
> *Is nailed to His cross and I bear it no more.*
> *Praise the Lord, praise the Lord, O my soul!*
> —HORATIO G. SPAFFORD

It includes both the forgiveness of transgressions and the cleansing of the principle of sin (the self-centeredness that lies behind all overt disobedience and remains as a "broken power" even in those who are regenerate). This means that for Wesleyan theology, the Atonement includes both reconciliation (or justification) and sanctification.

How does the work of Christ effect these results? Wesley's best answer is in terms of the threefold office of Christ, as Prophet, Priest, and King. In this way the narrow focus of the classical theories upon the death of Christ so as not to take into account the whole Christ-event is avoided. In his note on Phil. 3:8, Wesley describes Christ as Prophet, Priest, and King "as teaching me wisdom, atoning for my sins, and reigning in my heart. To refer this to justification only is miserably to pervert the whole scope of the words. They manifestly relate to sanctification also; yea, to that chiefly."

As *Prophet,* Christ is the Revealer of the nature of God. His ministry, which freely offered forgiveness and healing to those who were needy and acknowledged it, witnessed to the love of God, which reached out to the lost, the last, and the least (see Luke 15). At the same time He was the Revelation of human nature as

God intended it should be in His creative purpose. In this sense Jesus is the ideal man, the perfect reflection of the image of God in human existence. Since the purpose of the law is also to call man to full humanness, Jesus is the Fulfillment (end) of the law and embodies it perfectly.

As *Priest*, Jesus is the Mediator between God and man. Only the Book of Hebrews develops the priestly office explicitly, but many of its essential functions are found elsewhere. As a go-between or bridge builder, the priest must have a relation to both parties whom he is bringing together. Hence Hebrews in particular lays especially stress upon both His full deity (1:3-14) and His full humanity (5:1-8).

In order to carry out His priestly function, Jesus completely identified himself with humanity. The Incarnation was the crucial moment in this identification, but at every stage in His life He implements a specific facet of His union with man's predicament: His baptism, His temptation, His suffering, but particularly in His death. Since death is the indisputable evidence of human fallenness (Romans 5) and the most poignant symbol of separation from God, Jesus' dying on the Cross was His existential experience of sin's most empirical devastation wrought upon the human spirit. Thus the cry of dereliction from the Cross was the expression of His total involvement in man's sinfulness. It is contrary to the central claims of the New Testament to say that God had actually abandoned His Son at this point; but like the Psalmist, quoted by Jesus, the depths of His condition resulted in a sense of desolation. But if "God was in Christ, reconciling the world unto himself" (2 Cor. 5:19), we have to say that at no point was the Father closer to the Son than at this moment.

In His priestly function of offering himself as a sacrifice for sins (a distinctly priestly activity) Jesus was dying for us. The *for* here means "on behalf of," not "instead of."[1] It is thus an expression of love, not a satisfaction of abstract justice.

Not understanding the meaning of sacrifice in biblical theology, we have often inferred that the death of Christ was necessary to change God's attitude toward sinners, to placate His anger with us. This presupposes that the motive of the Atonement was wrath, not love.

Sometimes our preaching leaves the wrong impression. A lit-

1. *God, Man, and Salvation*, 386-88.

tle girl returned from church, declaring, "I love Jesus, but I hate God!" Pressed by her mother, she explained, "God was mad at us; but Jesus loved us and died for us. Now God isn't mad at us anymore. I love Jesus, but I hate God!" Our so-called orthodox teaching does sometimes seemingly give this impression—that it took the death of Jesus to change God from a wrathful to a loving Being.

What does the Bible teach about this? Both the Old and New Testaments make one point absolutely clear: *Atonement is the act of God the Father.* The blood sacrifices of the Old Testament were not offered to placate a vengeful Deity. No, *God himself* instituted the sacrificial system. Listen to the law: "For the life of the flesh is in the blood; and *I have given it for you* upon the altar to make atonement for your souls" (Lev. 17:11, RSV, italics added). It is God, the injured party, who makes atonement for man, the sinner. *He* provides the sacrifice—to show the seriousness and deadliness of sin and to cleanse the sinner's conscience of the stain of guilt as he receives God's promise of pardon.

God's initiative and action in atonement is the presupposition of every New Testament text on the subject. Paul writes of "Christ Jesus: whom *God* hath set forth to be a propitiation through faith in his blood" (Rom. 3:24-25). Again he says, "All things are of *God,* who hath reconciled us to himself by Jesus Christ" (2 Cor. 5:18; emphases added). He puts the matter beyond all doubt when he says in verse 19: "God was in Christ, reconciling the world unto himself." And John further declares, "Herein is love, not that we loved God, but that he loved us, and sent his Son to be the propitiation for our sins" (1 John 4:10).

"God is love—why atone?" the critic asks. "God has atoned—what love!" the Bible responds. The suffering God himself assumed our place because of our sin; this is the New Testament note.

The satisfaction theories of the Atonement fall short of the basic New Testament truth at this very point. The way they explain the work of Christ, it ends up by being the work of man: Christ as *man* offers satisfaction to God. If we remain true to the central thrust of biblical faith, we must avoid the suggestion that Jesus' death thus placates the Father God.

As *King,* Christ desires to reign in our hearts, in the present age and not simply in the age to come, as Sovereign. In this function, He furthermore represented us at the Cross by entering into mortal combat with demonic powers and overcame them, leading them in a parade of disgrace for all to behold their humiliation (Col. 2:15). With their defeat, their hold on humanity was broken, and men were potentially set free. It is to this aspect of the work of the Atonement that Gustav Aulen's *Christus Victor* motif speaks with telling force.

What Is Atonement?

The Atonement is the act of God in Christ that breaks down all the barriers our rebellion and sin have erected between the Father and ourselves. Sin has stabbed the heart of God with holy grief, because it has separated us from His loving fellowship. Not only has sin separated us from God, but also it has defiled our human nature and existence.

The Atonement means that as the offended party, the Father has taken our sin and guilt into His own heart by becoming our Reconciler in Christ, just as a spouse who has been sinned against and deeply hurt by a faithless companion assumes the shame and hurt of the other's sin by saying, "I love you and forgive you; and I am willing to help you find yourself again. Let us be reconciled."

This analogy probably comes as close as an illustration from human experience can to touching the heart of what the Atonement is. Although God has been sinned against, He bears that sin in His own heart. Forgiveness is not a flippant matter. The poet who said when dying, "Of course God will forgive me; that's His business!" never knew the deep pain that accompanies forgiving a loved one whose sin has wounded one's heart. God, who loves perfectly, suffers most deeply by forgiving His rebel creature. A cross has been in the heart of God from all eternity. The crucifixion of Christ was the historical moment of God's eternal sin-bearing.

A dramatic painting hangs in the Louvre. As one comes upon it, it seems to be a mere blending of shadows and darkness. Nothing seems to break the unrelieved darkness. As the observer draws closer, he sees vaguely the outline of a Cross hidden behind the veil of shadows. Then, as one looks longer, he becomes strangely aware that behind the Cross are the dim outlines of a Figure with hands outstretched, holding the Cross; and the agony on the Face behind the Cross is more terrible than the agony on the face of Him pinioned on the tree. The Cross reveals the heart of God. It does not change God, it discloses what He has been from "before the foundation of the world" (Eph. 1:3-7). The Cross that was erected on Calvary has been from eternity in the heart of God.

God the Father, in His Son Jesus Christ, has assumed our sin and guilt. The Father is in the Son, as the Son is in the Father. Therefore, when we read that God made Christ an atoning Sacrifice for the sins of the world, we understand that if possible, He suffered an even greater agony and loss than Jesus dying upon the Cross. Think of what agony Abraham would have suffered had God not stayed His hand on Mount Moriah, as he was about to sacrifice his only son Isaac! What God would not permit Abraham to do, He himself has done—for us! He offered up His own Son to die in our behalf—and it broke His heart!

How Do We Receive Atonement?

We "joy in God through our Lord Jesus Christ," Paul writes, "by whom we have now received the atonement" (Rom. 5:11). The Atonement is God's act in Christ on our behalf. How do we receive the benefits it makes available?

The gospel answer is so simple many are offended: *Believe!* To be saved, believe with Paul: "The Son of God . . . loved me, and gave himself for me" (Gal. 2:20).

"Who is this 'me'?" Luther asks. "I, wretched and damnable sinner, dearly beloved of the Son of God." If I could be saved by any other means, the Son of God would not have died. "Read the words 'me' and 'for me' with great emphasis," Luther counsels. "Print this 'me' with capital letters in your heart, and do not ever doubt that you belong to the number of those who are meant by this 'me.' . . . If we cannot doubt that we are sinners, we cannot deny that Christ died for our sins."

It is believing that Jesus loves me that melts my heart to repentance. And trusting His sacrifice for my sins, my conscience is cleansed. The guilt of sin is canceled, and the power of sin is broken! "Therefore being justified by faith, we have peace with God through our Lord Jesus Christ" (Rom. 5:1). *This* is "at-one-ment" with God!

My "at-one-ment" with God, however, is not total until my personal identification with the Cross is complete. "So long as Christ and I are two," Luther confessed, "I am undone." As Christ's identification with sinful man was total, in His incarnation and His death, so my identification must be without reservation, "becoming like him in his death" (Phil. 3:10, RSV). The full meaning of the Atonement, therefore, is not realized until I can say with Paul,

"I have been crucified with Christ; it is no longer I who live, but Christ who lives in me" (Gal. 2:20, RSV). In this total identification, the Atonement means full sanctification, the annulment of self-sovereignty and its replacement by Jesus Christ as personal Lord.

Suggested Additional Reading

Gustav Aulen, *Christus Victor.*
Donald M. Baillie, *God Was in Christ,* chaps. 7—8.
James Denney, *The Death of Christ.*
H. Ray Dunning, "Sacrifice," *Beacon Dictionary of Theology,* 466-67.
J. Glenn Gould, *The Precious Blood of Christ.*
J. Kenneth Grider, "Atonement," *Beacon Dictionary of Theology,* 54-55.
J. S. Whale, *Christian Doctrine,* chap. 4.

6

Divine Grace and Human Response

In the two previous chapters we have laid the groundwork for a discussion of how the work of God in Christ is to be brought to bear on the human predicament. This is not a peripheral question but is the focal point of the issues of original sin and salvation. Dwight L. Moody is often quoted as saying, "All the theology one needs to know to be saved is that I am a sinner and Christ is the Savior." But this is only two-thirds of the necessary knowledge; one also must know how these two realities are brought together, and it makes a tremendous difference how one answers the question.

Throughout history, theological thought has oscillated back and forth between emphasis on first one and then the other of the two truths of divine grace and human response. As with most issues, the truth would seem to lie in a balance between them. Wesleyan theology follows this middle course in its classic expression.

In the early centuries of the Christian movement, theological work was largely done under the dominance of Greek thought, and the idea of human freedom was never questioned. It was simply assumed that men were free to respond to the gospel offer. This is the same thing as saying that these early thinkers (for example,

Justin Martyr, Irenaeus, Origen, et al.) did not develop much of a doctrine of original sin. Certain Latin fathers did teach it and oftentimes in a rather extreme form.

The issue came to be vigorously discussed in the fifth century in a debate between Augustine and Pelagius. Concerned over the moral implications of emphasizing the inevitability of sin, Pelagius repudiated the idea that sin is unavoidable because man is born corrupt. As noted earlier, he argued that each man is his own Adam with a perfectly free will to decide the direction his life would take.

Pelagius did not jettison the idea of grace, however, but interpreted it in a way consistent with his own understanding of sin. Free will itself is grace. So also is the example of Christ as well as His teaching on the law. This placed the responsibility for man's moral development squarely upon his own shoulders and made it impossible to hide behind a view of the inescapability of sin.

However, the main movement of Christian thought followed Augustine in rejecting this optimistic view of human nature and such external understanding of grace. Augustine insisted that knowing the truth was not sufficient; the will was so perverted that man's condition was *non posse non peccare* (not possible not to sin). What he must have is internal grace, healing the will.

But in Augustine's polemical emphasis on grace, he so exclusivized it that he fostered the idea of predestination. This was a consequence of developing a "logical" doctrine of salvation by sovereign grace. If it is "grace alone" and only some men respond to the gospel, it seems logically to follow that grace is extended to only a select few, not all.

The development in Catholic thought during the succeeding centuries moved back in the direction of Pelagianism. Coming to fullest expression in the teaching of Thomas Aquinas, the standard view was that man enjoyed a twofold status corresponding to the "image" and the "likeness" of God.[1] In the Fall, the "likeness" was lost, very much like removing the second floor of a two-storied building, but the "image" remained unimpaired. The "first floor" then provided the basis for man's approach to God intellectually, ethically, and savingly. Salvation only involved the addition of a

---

1. This distinction roots back in Irenaeus and is the result of failing to recognize Hebrew parallelism, a form of Hebrew idiom that repeated the same idea twice, rather than stating two different meanings.

donum superadditum (superadded gift) to an already good substructure.

In the Protestant Reformation, Martin Luther rejected all this because it was one of the theological bases of the Catholic doctrine of works. Luther insisted that the whole program collapsed because it assumed that man could offer works that were acceptable to God, whereas man before God *(coram Deo)* is so totally corrupt that "all his virtues are but splendid vices."[2] Even the good things he did made no contribution to his salvation because they were done outside of faith, which was the exclusive gift of grace.

Here the pendulum swung too far in the opposite direction and in reaction to the humanism of Catholicism, Luther virtually denied free will to man in relation to God and thus ended up with predestination. John Calvin followed suit and systematized these ideas in his famous *Institutes of the Christian Religion.* It is the name of Calvin that is usually associated with the predestinarian doctrine. One must keep in mind, however, that *unconditional election and absolute predestination* served for the Reformers as the final and decisive bulwark against and rejection of the Catholic doctrine of salvation by good works.

We can now see, in this very cursory way, how Christian thought has demonstrated a movement between the two poles of divine grace and human response. John Wesley, in the 18th century, developed an understanding that moved between them without losing sight of either. The clue to his teaching is in the doctrine of *prevenient grace.*

Wesley concurred with those theologians in the Augustinian tradition regarding the totally depraved condition of the human race. None ever took original sin more seriously than he. Natural man has *within himself* no possibility of reaching out to God, no freedom in relation to God. This leaves the matter of salvation solely up to the grace of God. But the uniqueness here is that such a *natural man* is a "logical abstraction." There is no such thing as a natural man; no one is totally devoid of grace "unless he has quenched the Spirit."

This grace that goes before (prevenient or "preventing" grace) grants man the *gracious ability* to respond to the call of the gospel; but—and this distinguishes Wesley from Calvin—man is also capable of rejecting this call in the abuse of his freedom. Wesley

---

2. A quote that came from Augustine and was reiterated by Wesley.

himself said he was but a "hair's breadth" from Calvinism, and it is prevenient grace that provides the "hair."

Our salvation is by divine grace, not by human endeavor. This means two things: First, our salvation is by God's gracious provision in the cross of Jesus. This is "objective" grace, sometimes defined as God's unmerited favor in Christ. Second, our salvation is by God's gracious assistance through the Holy Spirit. This may be termed "subjective" grace: God at work within our hearts awakening, convicting, converting, cleansing us. It was this dual meaning of grace of which John Wesley was thinking when he said that God's grace is "free *for* all, and free *in* all."

Salvation is by grace alone, not by works. Nevertheless we cannot be saved without freely responding to God. As Augustine remarked, "He who made us without ourselves, will not save us without ourselves."[3] Man cannot save himself, but in order to be saved he must "do" something: he must "believe on the Lord Jesus Christ" (Acts 16:31). God takes the initiative in our salvation. He provides Christ as the perfect Sin Offering and calls us to himself by the Spirit, but we must respond in penitent, obedient trust in order to be saved. Yet even this faith that saves is by the gracious ability the Spirit gives. "As all merit is in the Son of God, in what He has done and suffered for us," writes Wesley, "so all power is in the Spirit of God."[4]

The Divine Working

One of John Wesley's most important sermons was titled "On Working Out Our Own Salvation." His text was Phil. 2:12-13: "Work out your own salvation with fear and trembling. For it is God which worketh in you both to will and to do of his good pleasure."

"First," says Wesley, "we are to observe that great and important truth which ought never to be out of our remembrance: 'It is God that worketh in us both to will and to do of his good pleasure.'" This statement "removes all imagination of merit from man and gives God the whole glory of His work."

Then Wesley makes a discerning observation on this text. "The expression is capable of two interpretations; both of which are

---

3. As with many issues Augustine speaks on both sides of the question.
4. "A Farther Appeal to Men of Reason and Religion," in *Works of John Wesley* 8:49.

unquestionably true. First, *to will* may include the whole of inward, *to do*, the whole of outward, religion. And if it be thus understood, it implies, that it is God that worketh both inward and outward holiness. Secondly, *to will* may imply every good desire; *to do*, whatever results therefrom. And then the sentence means, God breathes into us every good desire, and brings every good desire to good effect."[5]

On the basis of this faith knowledge we can affirm with Paul, "I am confident of this very thing, that He who began a good work in you will perfect it until the day of Christ Jesus" (Phil. 1:6, NASB).

The Human Working

What connection, however, is there between the two parts of Phil. 2:12 and 13? "If it is God that worketh in us both to will and to do, what need is there of our working?" Wesley asks. He calls this objection "the reasoning of flesh and blood." If we really consider what Paul is saying, we see the relationship between God's working and ours. The text really means, says Wesley, "First, God works; therefore you *can* work: Secondly, God works, therefore you *must* work.

"First. God worketh in you; therefore, you *can* work." If God did not work in us, it would be impossible to work out our own salvation. It is as impossible for us, who are "dead in trespasses and sins" (Eph. 2:1), to do anything for our salvation as it was impossible for Lazarus to come forth until the Lord had given him life. "It is equally impossible for us to *come* out of our sins, yea, or to make the least motion toward it, till He who hath all power in heaven and earth calls our dead souls into life."[6]

Yet this offers no one the excuse for continuing in sin by rationalizing, "It is God only that must quicken us; for we cannot quicken our own souls." Notice Wesley's famous answer:

> Allowing that all the souls of men are dead in sin by *nature*, this excuses none, seeing there is no man that is in a state of mere nature; there is no man, unless he has quenched the Spirit, that is wholly void of the grace of God. No man living is entirely destitute of what is vulgarly called *natural conscience*. But this is not natural: It is more properly termed, *preventing grace*. Every man has a greater or less measure of this, which

waiteth not for the call of man. . . . So that no man sins because he has not grace, but because he does not use the grace which he hath.

Therefore, inasmuch as God works in you, you are now able to work out your own salvation. . . . We know, indeed, that word of His to be absolutely true: "Without me ye can do nothing." But, on the other hand, we know, every believer can say, "I can do all things through Christ that strengtheneth me." . . . You can do something, through Christ strengthening you. Stir up the spark of grace which is now in you, and He will give you more grace.

Secondly. God worketh in you; therefore, you *must* work. You must be "workers together with him," (they are the very words of the Apostle,) otherwise He will cease working. . . . [It is here that Wesley quotes Augustine:] "He that made us without ourselves, will not save us without ourselves." He will not save us unless we "save ourselves from this untoward generation;" unless we ourselves "fight the good fight of faith, and lay hold on eternal life;" unless we "agonize to enter in at the strait gate," "deny ourselves, and take up our cross daily," and labour by every possible means to "make our own calling and election sure."

. . . Go on, in virtue of the grace of God, preventing, accompanying, and following you, in "the work of faith, in the patience of hope, and the labour of love." "Be ye steadfast and immovable, always abounding in the work of the Lord." And "the God of peace, who brought again from the dead the great Shepherd of his sheep," (Jesus) "make you perfect in every good work to do his will, working in you what is well-pleasing in his sight, through Jesus Christ; to whom be glory for ever and ever!"[7]

On the basis of this possible and necessary working of the believer with God we must balance Phil. 1:6, quoted above, with another text from Paul: "And you, that were sometime alienated and enemies in your mind by wicked works, yet now hath he reconciled in the body of his flesh through death, to present you holy and unblameable and unreproveable in his sight: if ye continue in the faith grounded and settled, and be not moved away from the hope of the gospel" (Col. 1:21-23). Our salvation is wholly by God's grace, but Paul cautions us all when he warns the Corinthians, "We then, as workers together with him, beseech you also that ye receive not the grace of God in vain" (2 Cor. 6:1).

---

7. Ibid., 512-13.

The Paradox of Christian Experience

When these theological ideas are actualized in experience, they result in an intuition that is paradoxical in nature. Donald Baillie has summarized it in the following words:

> Its essence lies in the conviction which a Christian man possesses, that every good thing in him, every good thing he does, is somehow not wrought by himself but by God. This is a highly paradoxical conviction, for in ascribing all to God it does not abrogate human personality nor disclaim human responsibility. Never is human action more truly and fully personal, never does the agent feel more perfectly free, than in those moments of which he can say as a Christian that whatever good was in them was not his but God's.[8]

This experience is a direct intuition that when I do wrong, I feel myself to be responsible, and I am condemned by conscience. Yet, strangely enough, when I do the right, I am not given approval by my conscience so that I have a feeling of self-esteem. Grace and personal responsibility so intersect that it is impossible to draw boundaries around each so that we can state precisely where one ends and the other begins. It is as Jonathan Edwards is reported as saying: "It is all of God, it is all of men."

This expression may be found in the great devotional literature throughout the centuries. While it may not be susceptible to a completely rational explanation, it nonetheless is the outcome of a distinctly Christian experience of God.

It is this that gives the unique character to Christian ethics. In fact, some have suggested that there is no such thing as a Christian ethic because Christian behavior is a response to grace. Unlike certain moral philosophies, the Christian faith does not teach that men become good by doing good. The goodness they possess is derived solely from God alone. As a familiar hymn puts it:

> And every virtue we possess
> And every victory won
> And every thought of holiness
> Are His alone.
> —HARRIET AUBER

But this does not relieve the Christian from moral behavior. In

---

8. *God Was in Christ*, 114.

fact, the total dependence upon grace that is his immediate experience calls him to holiness, not as a way of earning God's favor or becoming moral, but as a way of pursuing man's chief end, which is to "glorify God—the cultivation of faith and love toward Him as He comes to us through our relationship with our fellow-creatures."[9]

Suggested Additional Reading

J. Kenneth Grider, "Prevenient Grace," *Beacon Dictionary of Theology*, 415-16.
Clark Pinnock, *Grace Unlimited.*
W. T. Purkiser, *Security: the False and the True.*
Mildred Wynkoop, *Foundations of Wesleyan-Arminian Theology.*

---

9. Ibid., 44; see 98-99.

PART **III**

The Christian Life

Salvation

"Salvation" is a theological term having very broad connotations. It encompasses the whole work of God directed toward restoring man to his lost estate. Beginning with initial salvation, it includes all aspects of that restoration up to and including final salvation or "glorification." The New Testament speaks of salvation in three tenses: past (have been), present (are being), and future (will be). Since salvation is concerned with God's relation to man, it properly belongs under the doctrine of the Holy Spirit as an aspect of a theological system.

The terms "salvation" and "to be saved" first appear in the Old Testament in connection with the Exodus and mean "to be wide, spacious, to be free." The deliverance from slavery thus gives content to the concept. To be saved means to be freed from bondage. In the New Testament, the political overtones present from this event are minimized, while the spiritual are maximized, and it comes to connote freedom from sin.

The Order of Salvation

The Christian Church seems to have focused on one problem at a time during its theological development. As issues arose through threats from false understandings that appeared to undermine the faith, theologians directed their attention toward those matters. In the earliest period, they moved from the question of the Old Testament, to the doctrine of Creation, to the debate over the deity of Christ (Trinitarian discussion), and then to the person of Christ (Christological discussion). At the time of the Protestant Reformation in the 16th century the burning issue became the *order of salvation,* or put differently, "What must I do to be saved?"

The two theological terms that occupied center stage in this debate were *justification* and *sanctification.* Justification implies being declared innocent or not guilty, and involves being accepted by God. Sanctification means to be made holy or freed from impurity. The debate concerned which was first in the order of salvation.

The Catholic position was that sanctification preceded justification. One must become holy before he is accepted by God. Thomas Aquinas gave classic expression to this view. According to Thomas, the Christian life began with *faith.* By faith, however, he meant mental assent to the teachings of the church. But this was only the initial step in the process of "being saved." Faith was not enough, it was only potentially salvific. It needed, in Thomas' famous formula, to be *"faith formed by love."* That is, one is saved by faith *and* love.

The Christian life, then, is a process of sanctification or growing in love through good works prescribed by the church. When this process was completed, and one was completely sanctified, he was justified. That is to say, God declared him to be righteous because he had become righteous by good works. The good Catholic was then ready for heaven.

This understanding raised problems. What if one died before his sanctification was finished? Since he could not get into heaven, there arose the belief in an intermediate state or place called *purgatory* where the Catholic could become holy by suffering and complete the unfinished task of attaining full holiness.

Such a teaching inevitably produced anxiety for sensitive persons like Martin Luther. He wanted to know God's acceptance, but he could never feel that he had enough love. Eventually, he said, he came to hate God because of the demands laid upon him that he could not meet.

Out of his own biblical studies as a university professor, he came to see that the New Testament taught just the opposite from his early training. *Justification precedes sanctification,* and one is declared righteous by God on the basis of *His love and grace,* not man's goodness. All man has to do is receive God's free offer in

Christ, and he is justified then and there by *faith alone*. As Luther put it so graphically: "God saves sinners."

In lieu of Aquinas' formula of "faith formed by love," Luther declared that the Christian life is best represented by the formula *"faith formed by Christ."* One look at the Cross in faith, and the guilt of sin with its penalty is removed. It is important to note that he also resurrected the New Testament concept of faith as *trust* as over against the idea of assent.

John Wesley accepted completely the Protestant view that men are justified by faith alone. One's eternal destiny is settled at the initial act of faith. However, he perceived that the Catholic emphasis on holiness was also supported by New Testament teaching, so he combined the two emphases and embodied them in the formula *"faith working by love,"* from Gal. 5:6. Sanctification is the cultivation of love in the Christian life as a response to the freely bestowed gift of eternal life, not an attempt to earn it. In this chapter we look at the facets of *initial salvation;* in the next chapter we look at the *subsequent* aspects of the doctrine of salvation, most generally designated by the term *sanctification.*

In the previous chapter we discussed the two sides of the divine-human encounter in their paradoxical interpenetration. For purposes of analysis, we now wish to examine each side of this paradox separately in its various facets. First we will speak of our situation.

The Human Response

The proper term to use of this truth is *response.* "I sought the Lord," Augustine stated, "because He had already found me." Everyone who knows Christ is aware that he has been found. Salvation is not something that he discovered on his own initiative, but "we love him, because he first loved us" (1 John 4:19).

The beginning of the salvation process occurs in an awakening experience. By the means of a sermon, a testimony, a song, or some providential occurrence, the Holy Spirit arouses the sinner, who is "dead in trespasses and sins" (Eph. 2:1), to his lost condition. When God reveals himself and speaks to human consciousness, the basis for the saving response is laid.

Seeking the Lord involves several actions: confession of sin, repentance, and faith. Each of these needs to be understood in the light of biblical theology.

Confession. The Greek word (ὁμολογεῖν) *(homologein),* which is translated "to confess," literally signifies "to say the same thing." We confess when we acknowledge what God already knows about us, when we acquiesce in God's judgment about us. Confession of sins is quite different from admission of guilt. One may allow that he has done wrong, yet never feel regret over it. He may even plead "guilty" before a bar of justice but not experience the remorse that accompanies real Christian confession. True confession grows out of a heart smitten by love.

Repentance. The Hebrew word for "repent" means "turn." "Turn ye, turn ye . . . for why will ye die?" the prophet cries (Ezek. 33:11). "Let the wicked forsake his way, and the unrighteous man his thoughts: and let him return unto the Lord, and he will have mercy upon him; and to our God, for he will abundantly pardon" (Isa. 55:7). A sinner must about-face to get right with God.

The Greek word translated "repent" means "think again." Evangelical repentance, beginning as true self-knowledge produced by the Holy Spirit, is a change of mind with respect to God, sin, and oneself. To "bring forth . . . fruits meet for repentance" (Matt. 3:8) involves the willingness to rectify the wrong one has committed against the Lord and one's fellows and to change one's manner of living. It means to reorient one's life about God and His righteous way.

The thief on the cross repented when he cried, "Lord, remember me when thou comest into thy kingdom." Awakened and convicted by God's Spirit, he called on the Lord for salvation. He had no opportunity to "bring forth . . . fruits meet for repentance" other than this plea. Yet Jesus responded, "To day shalt thou be with me in paradise" (Luke 23:42-43).

Not every Christian thinker supports the idea of the necessity of repentance as a preparatory step to salvation. It has been questioned as being a proper response to the initial call of the gospel on two grounds. The first reason is seen in the alteration made in the early Catholic sacrament of penance. Originally penance involved four steps: (1) contrition, (2) confession, (3) satisfaction, and (4) absolution. Later, it was suggested that contrition was a distinctly Christian attitude and that one who is in mortal sin cannot feel it; therefore contrition was changed to *attrition.* Attrition means simply being sorry that you are *caught,* while contrition is being truly sorry that you have *sinned.* For Roman Catholic theology, then, repentance is the practice of a Christian virtue not preparatory to justification.

Interestingly enough, John Calvin also viewed repentance as something to be practiced *within* the Christian life. In fact, he repeatedly and consistently emphasized that repentance is a central element in the "process" of sanctification. That is why Reformed Christians regularly confess their sins both in public and private prayer.

Others have raised a second objection, namely, that to call for repentance prior to justification jeopardizes the Protestant belief that salvation is *by faith alone*. This objection thinks that to make repentance a preparatory step to salvation is to turn it into a good work. It is this position that underlies many approaches to evangelism that stress "believe" and "accept" but say nothing about repentance. But in no way does the Wesleyan interpretation of repentance in the order of salvation make it a meritorious act.

Wesleyan thought, however, feels that it is biblical to call men to repent of their sins; at the same time it insists upon the *sola fide* principle of Protestantism. Faith alone is the condition of salvation; but because of the sinful nature of man, repentance is necessary before faith can be exercised. A sinner whose back is turned on God cannot trust Christ. One must, by emptying his hand through repentance, prepare to receive the free gift of grace.

Faith. The link between repentance and salvation is faith—trust in Christ and Christ alone. To believe is to call upon the name of the Lord, as the dying thief did. To believe is to rest in the promise of Christ: "Him that cometh to me I will in no wise cast out" (John 6:37). To believe is to put one's whole weight down upon Christ, to trust the merits of His life, death, and resurrection. In John Wesley's words, it is "a reliance upon . . . Christ as *given for us,* and *living in us;* and in consequence . . . a closing with Him, and cleaving to Him, as our 'wisdom, righteousness, sanctification, and redemption', or in one word, our salvation."[1] All that precedes this act of faith, such as repentance, is but a clearing of the ground for this final closing with Christ. The Lord alone saves. Giving glory to God alone, faith gratefully receives the gift of salvation (see Rom. 4:20-25).

---

1. "Salvation by Faith," in *Standard Sermons* 1:40-41.

The Divine Act

As hinted at in the previous section, it is neither repentance nor faith that saves us. Salvation is much like an electric current that requires both a negative and a positive pole before the circuit is closed and the light bulb comes on. The human response is essential, but God must "close the circuit" by a divine saving act before one can truly say he is saved. It is a *divine-human* encounter.

The salvation that God bestows through Christ on the penitent, believing sinner is viewed in several ways in the New Testament. First, to believe in Christ is to be justified. To be justified means that, through my trust in Christ and His atoning death, I stand before God "just-as-if-I'd" never sinned! In the simplest terms, it means pardon through the blood of Jesus and acceptance with God.

Justification is a legal metaphor and derives from the procedures of a court of law. God is the Judge who pronounces the verdict regarding the accused. If the evidence is inadequate to demonstrate guilt, the judge rightfully and justly declares the accused to be "not guilty" (justified). But if the evidence demonstrates beyond any doubt that the culprit is guilty as accused, and then the judge declares him innocent, it is thought to be a scandal from the perspective of justice. That is why Paul points to the work of Christ as the ground of the possibility of God being both "just, and the justifier of him which believeth in Jesus" (Rom. 3:26).

The significance of this is that the Judge himself (in Christ) bears the guilt in His own heart and suffers the scandal so as to be free to pronounce the prisoner "not guilty." A failure to understand that the Judge is the Sin-bearer and that we are not dealing with some abstract law that must be satisfied leads to a perverted view of both God and the atoning work of Christ, as in certain satisfaction theories of the Atonement.

Justification issues in *reconciliation*. "Therefore being justified by faith, we have peace with God through our Lord Jesus Christ" (Rom. 5:1). By justification we are relieved of the *guilt* of sin; by reconciliation, of its *enmity*.

Reconciliation can doubtless be referred to as the primary metaphor in the divine-human relation. The term translated "atonement" in the New Testament (only in Rom. 5:11) can equally well be rendered as "reconciliation" and is in most modern versions. The reason it is primary is that it is derived from the realm of human relations, the domestic scene. This more adequately mirrors the issues at stake in salvation, and other metaphors must be made subservient to this perspective.

Much misunderstanding has arisen over the work of Christ by elevating the legal metaphors (e.g., justification) to the decisive level rather than interpreting them in personal terms. This has been somewhat inevitable due to the fact that (1) Western theology was originally developed out of Roman society, which was law oriented; and (2) some of the most influential theorists in Atonement theology were lawyers. Tertullian, a lawyer, has exercised a massive but sometimes unsuspected influence upon Western theology on this and other matters. John Wesley, with sure insights, demonstrated a strong affinity to Eastern Christendom with its more mystical and personal emphasis.

It needs to be noted also in this regard that it is man who is reconciled to God, not vice versa. Man is the rebel, the enemy; and his sin (self-will) stands as the barrier to salvation. God, like the father of the prodigal son, is always willing to accept the returning son when that son "comes to himself," swallows his pride, and returns to the Father (Luke 15:17-20). Paul stresses this point when describing the work of the ambassador for Christ whose message is "Be ye reconciled to God" (2 Cor. 5:20).

At the same instant a repentant sinner is justified and reconciled to God, he receives *adoption* into God's family. "And because ye are sons, God hath sent forth the Spirit of his Son into your hearts, crying, Abba, Father. Wherefore thou art no more a servant, but a son; and if a son, then an heir of God through Christ" (Gal. 4:6-7; cf. Rom. 8:14-17). "The Spirit [himself] beareth witness with our spirit, that we are the children of God" (Rom. 8:16). The divine Spirit assures him that he is now a child of God and puts within his heart the cry, "Father, dear Father!" with the same spontaneity a little baby says, "Abba!" or "Daddy!"

Furthermore, at the same moment he is justified, reconciled, and adopted, he is born of the Spirit, regenerated by the power of God. He is born again! A newborn babe begins to breathe, to cry, to see, and to hear. Likewise, the newborn believer receives the breath of the Spirit and cries to God. His eyes are now opened to behold the face of God in Jesus Christ, and his ears are unsealed to hear the voice of God in His Word!

The New Man

Up to this point our analysis of salvation could be interpreted in exclusively individualistic terms. But from the point of view of biblical faith, this would be a perversion. While salvation requires a personal response, and each one must in grace make his own decision, salvation makes one a part of a new order, a new community, a new age.

New Testament theology is structured in the light of a perspective that comes to expression throughout the whole of the Testament and can be considered the central motif of it. This is the idea that roots in Jewish apocalyptic thought of *two ages:* the present age, which is evil, and the age to come, which is the Kingdom Age.

The New Testament writers take the position that while the present age has not passed away, as Jewish apocalypticists thought would be necessary, it has been invaded by the age to come, and so the two exist contemporaneously. Thus the new order has broken into the old order and signaled its ultimate abolishment. Men either live in the present age under the control of Satan—the "god of this age" (2 Cor. 4:4, NIV)—and demonic powers, or else they are a part of the new age or order, or what is the same thing, the kingdom of God.

It is this cosmic significance that is in Paul's mind when he asserts, "If anyone is in Christ, he is a new creation; the old has gone, the new has come!" (2 Cor. 5:17, NIV). The old age has passed away, and the new age has emerged; and he who is in Christ has become a part of the new. To believe in Christ, Paul teaches, is to pass out of the old creation into the new. When Jesus died, the old creation died (provisionally) with Him; when He arose, the new creation came (provisionally) into being. To believe in Christ is to enter into His death and resurrection and become part of the new creation He instituted.

The new man is thus a *corporate* reality. While anyone who has experienced the transforming grace of Christ in his own life can testify to "newness of life" (Rom. 6:4), it is also central to biblical faith that he is a part of a new race. The contours of this new reality (man) are described by Paul in Eph. 2:11-15.

Suggested Additional Reading

David Hill, *Greek Words and Hebrew Meanings: Studies in the Semantics of Soteriological Terms.*

E. Stanley Jones, *Conversion.*

Salvation, ed. John E. Hartley and R. Larry Shelton, vol. 1 of *Wesleyan Theological Perspectives.*

R. Larry Shelton, "Initial Salvation," *A Contemporary Wesleyan Theology* 1:473-516.

James S. Stewart, *A Man in Christ.*

George Allen Turner, "Salvation," *Beacon Dictionary of Theology,* 468-69.

Sanctification

"Sanctification" is a big word that confuses a lot of people, but it is the translation of a concept that is in the very warp and woof of biblical revelation. It is a correlative to the more basic word translated "holiness." We will first look at the meaning of the latter term in order to come to a better understanding of sanctification.

The Hebrew word *qodesh*, rendered in English as "holy," originally meant "separate" and was applied primarily to God. It was a way of speaking of that which is distinctly divine. God's holiness distinguishes Him from, sets Him apart from, all finite reality. Men and objects or places may become "holy" in a derivative sense by being connected in some way with God, such as being His property or the place where He has revealed himself or some such association.

The act or process by which finite objects become "holy" is referred to as "sanctification." To sanctify, we might say, is to "holify." Particularly in the Old Testament certain rituals were specified by which this would occur. In this setting, one should qualify the term "sanctification" with *ceremonial*. Ceremonial holiness or sanctification conveys the quality of "belonging to God" by either contact or an act of dedication.

Ceremonial holiness did not necessarily suggest any ethical content. In fact, one finds the rather startling reference in the Old Testament to "holy prostitutes." However, in Israel, the ethical element soon emerged as a distinctive emphasis and was given explicit expression by the prophets. For this reason, scholars have spoken of *prophetic holiness* to describe the understanding of holiness that is ethical in nature.

Although Jesus made reference to ceremonial sanctification (Matt. 23:17, 19), He quite clearly stood in the mainstream of the prophetic doctrine. Paul develops this understanding as it relates to Christian experience, and so the Christian doctrine of sanctification usually is drawn from the Epistles. It is there that the application of "holiness" language to life is most clearly used and always with an ethical connotation.

In developing the idea of sanctification as an aspect of the broader theme of salvation, it would be profitable to keep in mind John Wesley's lucid distinction between justification and sanctification: *Justification is a relative change, sanctification is a real change.* Utilizing this significant insight, which is theologically sound, we will be able to adequately explore the many-faceted uses of sanctification in doctrinal discussions.

Wesley's distinction assumes an ethical connotation to sanctification rather than ceremonial, consonant with the normative New Testament teaching. If a person or an object is sanctified ceremonially (set apart), it does not necessarily undergo any inherent (real) change. A person can submit to a ritual of purification but not experience any ethical transformation. But to comply with Wesley's definition of sanctification, such changes must occur.

By defining justification as a relative change, Wesley intends a change of relation. From the relation of guilt, it becomes a relation of innocence. Justification in and of itself does not involve a real change in the subject. This is why justification can be *logically* distinguished from sanctification even though there is no chronological distinction, as we will see later. Furthermore, it is why it can be demonstrated biblically and theologically that sanctification is logically subsequent to justification, because men are not accepted by God on the basis of their holiness but "just as they are." Thus justification is logically prior in the divine-human relationship (see previous chapter).

Based on Wesley's definition of sanctification as a real change, there are several metaphors of salvation that should be seen as subdivisions of the larger truth of sanctification: regeneration (new birth), growth in grace, and entire sanctification. If one restricts the use of the term to *entire* sanctification he will have difficulty understanding in context virtually all the uses of the term "sanctification" in the New Testament.

Regeneration. Regeneration in the sense here employed is not a biblical term but one that theologians coined to refer to what Jesus spoke of in one place as the new birth (John 3:3 ff.). It is intended to suggest that one who has been dead in sin has been given new life. This spiritual resurrection is a real change.

The quality of this new life that has been imparted is holy in nature. In spiritual matters, it is impossible to distinguish "life" from a "quality of life," as some have attempted to do. Wesley did not use the term *initial sanctification,* but his definitions imply that had he done so, he would have used it as a synonym for regeneration. This explains how it can be properly asserted that all Christians are sanctified, but not entirely. This means more than a ceremonially "belonging to God" by being "set apart." It marks a real transformation from death to life. Paul makes this clear when he addresses the Corinthian Christians as "sanctified in Christ Jesus and called to be holy" (1 Cor. 1:2, NIV). That he means this in an ethical sense is spelled out in 6:9-11: "Do you not know that the wicked will not inherit the kingdom of God? Do not be deceived: Neither the sexually immoral nor idolaters nor adulterers nor male prostitutes nor homosexual offenders nor thieves nor the greedy nor drunkards nor slanderers nor swindlers will inherit the kingdom of God. And that is what some of you were. But you were washed, *you were sanctified,* you were justified in the name of the Lord Jesus Christ and by the Spirit of our God" (NIV, italics added). But a careful reading of the whole letter leaves no doubt that they were not entirely sanctified.

Growth in Grace. If growth in grace is seen from a New Testament perspective, it too falls under the rubric of sanctification. The simplest definition for this phenomenon of Christian existence is *increasing conformity* to the Christ-pattern.

The clearest statement of what is involved in spiritual growth is found in 2 Pet. 3:18: "But grow in grace, and in the knowledge of our Lord and Saviour Jesus Christ." The correlative concepts of growth and knowledge are not incidentally related. As one comes to *know* Christ better, the grace of God through the Holy Spirit leads one to bring his life more and more into accord with Christ's pattern of living. A scrutiny of Paul's writings will reveal a significant emphasis on knowledge as essential to the developing Christian life with the same implications as in 2 Peter.

Entire Sanctification. While various aspects of sanctification were discussed with differing emphases throughout the history of Christian thought about the Christian life, it was John Wesley, in the 18th century, who recovered for the Church Universal the teaching of entire sanctification or Christian perfection. Referring to his brother Charles and himself, John records: "In 1729, two young men, reading the Bible, saw they could not be saved without holiness, followed after it, and incited others so to do."

One of the unique features of Wesley's teaching is that he defined the content of sanctification as being love. In doing so, he was in accord with a long tradition of teaching of Christian piety. Thus love is the initial experience of all born-again believers; it is the cultivation of love that is the genus of growth in grace, and it is the qualitative perfection of love that he identifies as entire sanctification, refusing to give any other content to it. Furthermore it is by defining it in terms of love that made it theologically possible for him to make the novel and enticing claim that such perfect love is attainable in this life.

Wesley's simplest summary of his doctrine is found in *A Plain Account of Christian Perfection.* In arguing that the experience of perfect love can be realized in this life, he points out:

"1. There is such a thing as perfection; for it is again and again mentioned in Scripture.

"2. It is not so early as justification; for justified persons are to 'go on unto perfection.'

"3. It is not so late as death; for St. Paul speaks of living men that were perfect."[1]

What Is Entire Sanctification?

On January 1, 1733, Wesley preached before Oxford University in St. Mary's Church on "The Circumcision of the Heart." He said of Christian perfection: "It is that habitual disposition of soul which, in the sacred writings, is termed holiness; and which directly implies the being cleansed from sin, 'from all filthiness both of flesh and spirit;' and, by consequence, the being endued with those vir-

---

1. (Kansas City: Beacon Hill Press of Kansas City, 1966), 114.

tues which were in Christ Jesus; the being so 'renewed by the image of our mind,' as to be 'perfect as our Father in heaven is perfect.'"[2]

Again, Wesley says: "The Gospel of Christ knows of no religion, but social; no holiness, but social holiness. *Faith working by love* is the length and breadth and depth and height of Christian perfection."[3]

Entire sanctification, Wesley taught, is neither more nor less than pure love—love expelling sin and governing both the heart and the life. "It is love excluding sin; love filling the heart, taking up the whole capacity of the soul. . . . For as long as love takes up the whole heart, what room is there for sin therein?"[4]

Anders Nygren speaks of Rom. 5:5 as Paul's version of Pentecost: "For the love of God has been poured out in our hearts through the Holy Spirit who has been given to us" (literal translation).

Colin Williams writes: "The great strength of Wesley's doctrine is in his awareness that the work of sanctification is a gift, a divine work wrought by God and to be accepted by faith. There is a gradual work of transformation issuing from the day-to-day relationship with Christ, and the need for this gradual transformation continues throughout life, but there is also the promise of the immediate gift of an unbroken relationship with Christ."[5]

Is Sanctification Crisis or Process?

This is Wesley's question: "Is this death to sin, and renewal in love, gradual or instantaneous?" His answer is classic:

> A man may be dying for some time; yet he does not, properly speaking, die, till the soul is separated from the body; and in that instant, he lives the life of eternity. In like manner, he may be dying to sin for some time; yet he is not dead to sin, till sin is separated from his soul; and in that instant, he lives the full life of love. And as the change undergone, when the body dies, is of a different kind, and infinitely greater than any we had known before, yea, such as till then, it is impossible to conceive; so the change wrought, when the soul dies to sin, is of a different kind, and infinitely greater than any before, and than

2. Ibid., 12.

3. *Poetical Works of John Wesley,* ed. George Osborne (London, 1838), 1: xxii. From preface to *Hymns and Sacred Poems,* 1739 hymnbook.

4. *Works* 6:46, 52.

5. *John Wesley's Theology Today* (London: Epworth Press, 1962), 186.

any can conceive, till he experiences it. Yet he still grows in grace, in the knowledge of Christ, in the love and image of God; and will do so, not only till death, but to all eternity.[6]

Toward the end of the *Plain Account* he records the objection: "But in some, this change was not instantaneous." Wesley answers: "They did not perceive the instant when it was wrought. It is often difficult to perceive the instant when a man dies; yet there is an instant in which life ceases. And if ever sin ceases, there must be a last moment of its existence, and a first moment of our deliverance from it."[7]

How Do We Wait for This Change?

Wesley gives this reply to his question "How are we to wait for this change?"

> Not in careless indifference, or indolent inactivity; but in vigorous, universal obedience, in a zealous keeping of all the commandments, in watchfulness and painfulness, in denying ourselves, and taking up our cross daily; as well as in earnest prayer and fasting, and a close attendance on all the ordinances of God. And if any man dream of attaining it any other way (yea, or of keeping it when it is attained, when he has received it even in the largest measure), he deceiveth his own soul. It is true, we receive it by simple faith; but God does not, will not, give that faith, unless we seek it with all diligence, in the way which He hath ordained.[8]

> *But may we not continue in peace and joy till we are perfected in love?*

> Certainly we may; for the kingdom of God is not divided against itself; therefore, let not believers be discouraged from "rejoicing in the Lord always." And yet we may be sensibly pained at the sinful nature that still remains in us. It is good for us to have a piercing sense of this, and a vehement desire to be delivered from it. But this should only incite us the more zealously to fly every moment to our strong Helper. . . . And when the sense of our sin most abounds, the sense of His love should much more abound.[9]

One of Wesley's most helpful sermons on this point is titled "Satan's Devices." He cautions:

---

6. *Plain Account*, 62.
7. Ibid., 115.
8. Ibid., 62.
9. Ibid., 63, in Wesley's sermon on Rom. 8:1.

> Our wise adversary endeavours to make our conviction of the necessity of perfect love an occasion of shaking our peace by doubts and fears [and] to weaken, if not destroy, our faith. ... But if we let go our faith, our filial confidence in a loving, pardoning God, our peace is at an end, the very foundation on which it stood being overthrown. ... whatever strikes at this, strikes at the very root of all holiness: ... [and] so far as it succeeds, tears up the very root of the whole work of God.[10]

"Pardoning love is at the root of it all," Wesley insists. To lose the sense of this is to fall under a cloud of condemnation. But thank God! "There is therefore now no condemnation to them which are in Christ Jesus, who walk not after the flesh, but after the Spirit" (Rom. 8:1), *even for remaining sin.* Those who are not yet sanctified wholly may scripturally "rejoice evermore" (1 Thess. 5: 16) in the pardoning love of God.

Going On to Perfection

While the justified believer who walks before God in trustful obedience is free from condemnation, even though inward sin remains, there is no place for laxity under the excuse "God will take care of it." Clarence Bence observes that the whole of Wesley's theological understanding can be found in his constant use of the command to "go on."

> The Christian life is a way to the Kingdom and every pilgrim on the way must keep moving onward through the various stages in the order of salvation, from repentance to new birth, to entire sanctification, and even beyond in growth in perfection. Wesley warns those who would relax that "it is impossible that any should retain what they receive, without improving it," without panting after holiness. Each must press on to the goal, and the goal is nothing short of perfection, purity of heart and life.[11]

Being a Christian is like riding a bicycle: To stop is to fall. But for the Christian who understands the *gospel* of sanctification, "going on" is not a matter of futile *human* striving; it is a matter of opening up one's life to the power and activity of God in the confidence that "he who hath begun a good work in you will perfect it until the day of Jesus Christ" (Phil. 1:6, Wesley's NT). In harmony with this Wiley points out that the exhortation to "go on unto

---

10. *Works* 6:36-37.

11. Clarence Bence, "The Wesleyan Syndrome," *Preacher's Magazine* 55, no. 2 (December, January, February, 1979-80): 54.

perfection" in Heb. 6:1 should properly be translated, "Let us *be borne* or *carried* on" to perfection (italics added). The verb is passive. While active means are not excluded, the verb indicates that perfection is a divine work. The picture is of "a ship under full sail before the wind." Westcott views this as a call for "personal surrender to an active influence. The power is working . . . we have only to yield ourselves to it."[12] This surrender to God's sanctifying power and activity has been spoken of as "the rest of faith." The faith that purifies the heart and perfects it in love is a moment of passivity when God acts, as we rest on His promise and provision. "There remaineth therefore a rest for the people of God. For he that hath entered into his rest hath himself also ceased from his works, as God did from his" (Heb. 4:9-10, Wesley's NT).

In his sermon on "The Scripture Way of Salvation" Wesley delineates the faith that purifies the soul and perfects it in God's love.

> It is a divine evidence and conviction, first, that God hath promised it in the holy Scripture. Till we are thoroughly satisfied of this, there is no moving one step further. And one would imagine there needed not one word more to satisfy a reasonable man of this, than the ancient promise, "Then will I circumcise thy heart, and the heart of thy seed, to love the Lord thy God with all thy heart, and with all thy soul, and with all thy mind." How clearly does this express being perfected in love! —how strongly imply the being saved from all sin! For as long as love takes up the whole heart, what room is there for sin therein?
>
> It is a divine evidence and conviction, secondly, that what God hath promised He is able to perform. Admitting therefore, that "with men it is impossible" . . . to purify the heart from sin, and to fill it with all holiness; yet this creates no difficulty in the case, seeing "with God all things are possible." . . . If God speaks, it shall be done.
>
> It is, thirdly, a divine evidence and conviction that He is able and willing to do it now. And why not? Is not a moment to Him the same as a thousand years? He cannot want more time to accomplish whatever is His will. And He cannot want or stay for any more *worthiness* or *fitness* in the persons He is pleased to honour. We may therefore boldly say, at any point of time, "Now is the day of salvation!" . . .

12. Brooke Foss Westcott, *The Epistle to the Hebrews* (Grand Rapids: Wm. B. Eerdmans Publishing Co., [1955]), 143; quoted in H. Orton Wiley, *The Epistle to the Hebrews,* ed. Morris A. Weigelt, rev. ed. (Kansas City: Beacon Hill Press of Kansas City, 1984), 182.

To this confidence, that God is both able and willing to sanctify us now, there needs to be added one thing more,—a divine evidence and conviction that He doeth it. In that hour it is done: God says to the inmost soul, "According to thy faith be it unto thee!" Then the soul is pure from every spot of sin; it is clean "from all unrighteousness." The believer then experiences the deep meaning of those solemn words, "If we walk in the light as he is in the light, we have fellowship one with another, and the blood of Jesus Christ his Son cleanseth us from all sin."[13]

Suggested Additional Reading

Thomas Cook, *New Testament Holiness.*

Leo G. Cox, *John Wesley's Concept of Perfection.*

Wilbur T. Dayton, "Entire Sanctification," *A Contemporary Wesleyan Theology* 1:521-67.

W. M. Greathouse and Paul Bassett, *Exploring Christian Holiness*, vol. 2, *The Historical Development.*

Harald Lindström, *Wesley and Sanctification.*

W. T. Purkiser, "Sanctification," *Beacon Dictionary of Theology,* 469-70.

John Wesley, *A Plain Account of Christian Perfection.*

---

13. *Standard Sermons* 2:457-59.

The Church

After a study of salvation we turn now to explore more fully the corporate dimensions of salvation, which primarily means that while individuals are saved, they are not isolated units. Christianity is not an individualistic religion that sees persons as "atomic particles" unrelated to other individuals. As John Wesley said, "Christianity is essentially a social religion; and . . . to turn it into a solitary religion is indeed to destroy it."[1]

In the Early Church, there were no free-lance believers. When a person was converted to Christ, he was immediately incorporated by baptism into the visible gathering of Christ's Body, the Church. It was as simple as that. Just as in the Old Testament, salvation meant becoming a part of the people of God (Israel), so in the New it meant becoming associated with the rest of the believers who comprised the Church. Any other concept of salvation was inconceivable.

In time this New Testament faith and practice resulted in the doctrine that only in the *institutional* church is there salvation. By being baptized and partaking of the Lord's Supper, one was automatically a Christian. Institutional religion all but displaced vital Christianity. Then Luther and the Reformers rose up in protest and recovered the New Testament doctrine of salvation by personal

---

1. *Works* 5:296.

faith in Christ. John Wesley appeared later in England and preached the same Protestant message.

Neither the primary Reformers nor Wesley discarded the sacraments or the New Testament doctrine of the Church. Their preaching and teaching breathed new life into the Church and restored the sacraments to their biblical place. Yet out of their teaching grew a new brand of Pietism that set aside the New Testament teaching concerning the sacraments and the true nature of the Church. In this tradition, baptism and church membership became optional, and salvation tended to become a purely individualistic pursuit of piety and holiness.

What we need to see is that this individualistic kind of religion is not New Testament Christianity, but rather a modern religion that owes more to the pagan Renaissance than to the Protestant Reformation! It is high time that we recover the New Testament doctrine of the Church.

New Testament writers employed several images to speak of this corporate reality. We will look at two of them.

The People of God

In the first place, the New Testament makes it clear that the Christian Church is now the true people of God, the new Israel. Those who have the faith of Abraham, not simply those who have his blood in their veins, are the true children of Abraham and heirs of the promises the Lord made to him (see Rom. 9:6-9). The Church as the *ecclesia*, the assembly of the called-out ones, began with Abraham's call in Genesis 12. And as Abraham was justified by faith in the word of promise, so we are justified by faith in Christ, God's Word of promise to all (Romans 4). Abraham was circumcised as a sign and a seal of the righteousness he had by faith, being uncircumcised (Rom. 4:9-13). We are baptized in/with water as the sign and seal that we are in Christ (6:3-4). But both Abraham and all who have his faith are members of the one true people of God, which has existed in an unbroken chain since almost 2,000 years before Jesus.

This is why Peter can write to Christians in the Early Church and call them the *Diaspora*, God's elect people scattered over the face of the world (1 Pet. 1:1). This is why he could further say to them: "But you are a chosen people, a royal priesthood, a holy nation, a people belonging to God, that you may declare the praises of him who called you out of darkness into his wonderful light. Once you were not a people, but now you are the people of God" (2:9-10, NIV). These are almost the words of Exod. 19:5-6 and Deut. 7:6.

The New Testament declares that by the death and resurrection of Jesus "the middle wall of partition," which separated Jew and Gentile in the Israel of God, has been broken down forever in the Christian community that is the Body of Christ and the true temple of God (Eph. 2:11-22). The Old Testament taboos regarding diet and dress were all nailed to the Cross, along with the ceremonialism of the Law of Moses. Old Testament practices and sacrifices were but a "shadow of things to come; but the body is of Christ" (read Col. 2:9-23).

Ancient Israel was a national entity, identified by circumcision, the seventh-day Sabbath, and the ceremonial law. Jesus Christ has reconstituted Israel as a people of faith, a universal entity where "there is neither Jew nor Greek, there is neither bond nor free, there is neither male nor female: [but where they] are all one in Christ Jesus" (Gal. 3:28). "As many as walk according to this rule, peace be on them, and mercy, and upon the Israel of God" (6:16).

The Body of Christ

In the second place, the New Testament teaches that the Christian Church is the Body of Christ, the continuation of His presence and saving activity on earth. The Church is Christ's chosen way of being present in our world today. All that a man's body is to him, the Church is to Christ. As the man's body is the living, concrete expression of his true self—his invisible ego—the Church is the visible manifestation of the risen, glorified Christ.

The Church Universal is the one Body of Christ, of which the various denominations are so many historic manifestations, more or less faithful to His mind and Spirit. "There is one body and one Spirit—just as you were called to one hope when you were called—one Lord, one faith, one baptism; one God and Father of all, who is over all and through all and in all" (Eph. 4:4-6, NIV)—one Body, quickened and sanctified by one Spirit, saved and directed by one Head, the Lord Jesus Christ. "And God placed all things under his feet and appointed him to be head over everything for the church, which is his body, the fullness of him who fills everything in every way" (1:22-23, NIV).

Each congregation of baptized believers is a local body of Christ, the visible manifestation and *koinonia* of Christ in a given time and place (1 Cor. 12:12-13). The one Body of Christ manifests itself in local communions, and it is in the local fellowship of believers where Christ is savingly present and comfortingly near.

Christ embodies himself *universally* in that one great fellowship of all believers, "the communion of saints" that stretches backward to Jesus and the apostles and forward to the consummation of all things when the Lord shall return—that communion that embraces all men everywhere who are in Christ, both the living and the dead.

Christ embodies himself *locally* in each fellowship of Spirit-born, baptized believers who confess His name and worship Him in spirit and in truth. To any such body of believers Paul says, "Now ye are the body of Christ, and members in particular" (1 Cor. 12:27). Or, "For as we have many members in one body, and all members have not the same office: so we, being many, are one body in Christ, and every one members one of another" (Rom. 12:4-5).

Such an understanding defines sin for the Church. To those in the Corinthian church who were arguing that immorality is nothing, Paul writes, "Do you not know that your bodies are members of Christ himself? Shall I then take the members of Christ and unite them with a prostitute? Never! Do you not know that he who unites himself with a prostitute is one with her in body? For it is said, 'The two will become one flesh.' But he who unites himself with the Lord is one with him in spirit" (1 Cor. 6:15-17, NIV).

This defines sin not only in relation to the world but also within the Body of Christ. Within Christ's Body it is the spirit of independence that places my thoughts, my wishes, my personal glory in place of loving submission to the spirit of love or Christ's Spirit who dwells within His Body. (See 1 Cor. 12:12-27.)

Such an understanding of the Church also defines its mission: It is to continue the ministry of Jesus on earth (Acts 1:1; Luke 4:16-21). The risen Jesus still says to us as to the original disciples, "As my Father hath sent me, even so send I you" (John 20:21).

When we understand the Church in New Testament terms, we can agree with the ancient bishop who declared, "He who would have God for his Father must have the Church for his mother." Outside the biblical Church there *is* no salvation!

What Are the Marks of the Church?

The doctrine of the Church has proven to be a particularly thorny issue for Christian thinkers. Not the least of the reasons for this is the inevitable tendency of a church to become merely an institution. This gives birth to the problem of distinguishing between the institution as such and the true Church. One confusion that occurs in the minds of many has resulted in discussion of the church in sociological rather than theological terms.

The difficulty raised by institutionalization was the basis of Augustine's introduction into the stream of Christian thought of the distinction between the *visible* and the *invisible* church. Many theologians are calling this distinction into question today on the assumption that the term *invisible* implies that the Church is somehow not composed of flesh-and-blood people. However, no such meaning is intended in this discussion.

Within the context of the institutional church some such distinction is not only useful but necessary, just as it was necessary for Paul to write, "They are not all Israel, which are of Israel" (Rom. 9:6). The most casual observer will be forced to admit that if we take the New Testament seriously, denominations (taken collectively or separately) cannot be equated with the Church without remainder. This raises the theological question of the *marks of the Church.* What are the identifying characteristics of the *true* (invisible) Church? The answer to this question is implicit in the biblical images just surveyed and has undergone a historical development.

The first mark that could be mentioned, and probably the most primary, is that the Church is *constituted by the Spirit.* "Pentecost was the birthday of the Christian Church."[2] Membership in Israel as the people of God basically occurred through birth, but at Pentecost the people were brought together into a unique community by the activity of the Spirit. "The Church is the creation of the Holy Spirit."[3]

A careful analysis of the instances in the Book of Acts where a giving of the Spirit is recorded will show that in each case there is a close correlation between the reception of the Spirit and becoming visibly associated with the other local members of the Church. No individual as individual received the gift of the Spirit.

2. Wiley, *Christian Theology* 3:107.
3. Ibid.

This is the entailment of Paul's metaphor of the Church as the Body.

This continued to be understood as a mark of the Church into the early centuries of Christianity. Irenaeus, in the second century, writes: "Where the Church is, there is the Spirit of God; and where the Spirit of God is, there is the Church and all grace; and the Spirit is the truth. Those, therefore, who do not participate in the Spirit neither feed at their mother's breasts nor drink the bright fountain issuing from Christ's body."[4]

This emphasis on the Church as the unique sphere of the Spirit bore fruit quite different from its early meaning. When the Church was equated with the Roman Catholic institution, the process of domesticating the Spirit was complete. We hear Augustine insisting that the Holy Spirit is bestowed in the Church, by which he meant the Catholic church, and cannot be received outside the church. But this perversion does not invalidate the truth that Christ is Lord of the Church through the indwelling of the Spirit in Blood-bought believers who constitute the Church.

The other marks of the Church we might speak of are direct results of the first one just discussed. Very early there was an emphasis on the *unity* of the Church, which is a product of the Spirit. In the earliest days of postapostolic Christianity, the emphasis was laid on unity in terms of the faith inherited from the apostles. Even though it was scattered throughout the world, it shared the same truth. Irenaeus, for instance, supported this by maintaining that there was an unbroken succession of bishops going back to the apostles themselves, which guarantees that the faith of the church is identical to their original proclamation. Thus the term *apostolic* appears in this connection as a mark of the church. Cyprian develops this idea into its full expression that the principle of unity in the church is the bishop himself who is in the line of apostolic succession.

Today the Church still asserts its belief in its unity by its hymnody when it sings:

> *Like a mighty army Moves the Church of God.*
> *Brothers, we are treading Where the saints have trod.*
> *We are not divided; All one body we:*
> *One in hope and doctrine, One in charity.*
> —SABINE BARING-GOULD

4. *Against Heresies* 3.24.1.

But the realities of life cause us to wonder at this, because empirical Christianity certainly doesn't manifest these traits. Maybe we even sing it with tongue in cheek. If *unity,* or oneness, is a mark of the true Church, how can it be explained? H. Orton Wiley puts it this way: "The Scriptures nowhere speak of an outward or visible unity. There is no intimation of uniformity. . . . The unity is that of the Spirit; and the diversity includes anything that is not out of harmony with that spiritual unity."[5]

Universality was early considered a mark of the Church. This comes to expression in the creeds in the term *catholic,* which actually means universal. As with the concept of unity, the proliferation of Christendom into innumerable sects has jeopardized this trait unless it be treated in a spiritual sense and not related in any way to an institution.

The term *holy* found its way into the list of marks too. Again, however, various interpretations of this have been advanced. The sectarian view of the Church would identify the holiness of the Church with the holiness of its members. This tends to result in increased divisiveness and thus moves against certain other traits essential to the Church.

Certain theories suggest that the institution itself, apart from the individuals who make it up, is the bearer of holiness. Wiley proposes a via media between these two, saying that the holiness of the organization is in terms of the purpose and end for which it exists. The individuals have experienced a degree of holiness in their entrance into the benefits of the new covenant. This means that the holiness of the Church is both absolute and relative.

Defining the Church

To define the Church by a simple formula is very difficult, since "Church" is a complex reality. One major factor is the necessity of distinguishing a theological definition from all institutional organizations. The Church cannot be identified with any particular expression of it, but neither can it be completely separated from these. The history of efforts to identify marks of the Church testify to the complexity of the situation.

Wesleyan theology would not limit itself to any one mark of the Church as sufficient within itself to define the Church. It

---

5. *Christian Theology* 3:112.

would insist that the Church must be defined as both a saved and a saving community. This means that the Church has both nature and function. Both aspects are essential to the Church being the Church.

Wesley appeared to have given primacy to the characteristics of "living faith." This implies that the Church is composed of all spiritually regenerate persons, those who have entered into a vital relationship with Jesus Christ. But he would also insist on the importance of biblical preaching and the sacraments as critical in the life of the people of God. In addition, the element of discipline plays a significant role. This refers to the regulation of the ethical life of the people by the collective conscience. It takes all four of these traits, commonly called Protestant marks of the Church, to define the nature of the Church.

In addition, the Church must carry out the mission to which it is called. This mark goes back to Abraham, to whom the promise was given that through him the nations of the world would be blessed (Gen. 12:1-3). This mission was given to Israel, but since they failed to carry it out in a satisfactory way, the same mission was passed on to the New Israel, the Church. If the Church fails to carry out this divinely appointed mission, it becomes merely a religious club or a sect of the Pharisees.[6]

Suggested Additional Reading

The Church, ed. Melvin E. Dieter and Daniel N. Berg, vol. 4 of *Wesleyan Theological Perspectives*.

David L. Smith, "Ecclesiology," *A Contemporary Wesleyan Theology* 2:575-627.

Richard S. Taylor, "Church," *Beacon Dictionary of Theology*, 112-15.

David L. Watson, *I Believe in the Church*.

J. S. Whale, *Christian Doctrine*, chap. 6.

6. For a full development of these ideas, see H. Ray Dunning, "Toward a Wesleyan Ecclesiology," *Wesleyan Theological Journal* 22, no. 1 (Spring 1987): 111-17.

The Sacraments

Churches that lay primary stress upon individual religious experience tend to neglect the Christian sacraments. This is no doubt partly due to a reaction to *sacramentarianism,* the view that the sacraments automatically impart divine grace. But both of these stances are extreme and unbiblical. The nature of the Church demands that sacramental activities be observed and that they be personal in nature.

The Meaning of a Sacrament

The term *sacrament* is not found in the Bible but is taken from the Latin word *sacramentum,* which means "a consecrating." The idea of a sacrament is drawn from the fact that certain ceremonies or realities mediate the divine into human experience. When these become specific (or consecrated), they are established as continuing sacramental rites. Through them grace is somehow conveyed to the participant. That is why they are often termed *means of grace.*

Historically, three positions have been taken with respect to how this mediation is effected. Sacramentarianism, as mentioned above, is the doctrine that the sacraments actually convey divine grace, apart from any personal appropriation or ethical condition of the recipient *(ex opere operato).* This view is based on the assumption that the act is performed under divine authority by designated functionaries with the efficacy residing exclusively in the proper procedure and administering persons.

John the Baptist spoke against a similar if not identical understanding apparently present among the Pharisees who came to him to be baptized: "Produce fruit in keeping with repentance. And do not begin to say to yourselves, 'We have Abraham as our father.' For I tell you that out of these stones God can raise up children for Abraham" (Luke 3:8, NIV).

The opposite position is the teaching that the sacraments are only ordinances or rites symbolizing divine reality. In actuality, no grace is mediated at all, but the rites merely point to a prior encounter in which grace has been received. Such rites could properly be referred to as mere symbols.

A mediating position suggested here is an attempt to preserve the truth in each of these preceding views. While the sacramental act does not in and of itself mediate grace, nor is it efficacious *ex opere operato,* it is more than a sign. Grace may indeed be conveyed *contingent upon the faith of the recipient.* We believe that we are living in a sacramental universe. For those who have eyes to see, God is present and active in all about us. Likewise, for those who have faith, divine grace is operative in the sacraments. They do not operate automatically as vehicles of salvation, but they do become channels of grace for those who receive them as God intends them to be taken.

Based on the assumption that any ceremony authorized by the church can mediate grace, the Catholic position holds that there are seven sacraments: baptism, confirmation, Eucharist, penance, extreme unction, holy orders, and matrimony. The Protestant Reformers, Luther and Calvin, rejected all but two of these, based on a completely different definition of sacrament.

According to them, a sacrament is identified by two things: (1) an external sign, and (2) an accompanying promise of forgiveness. Only baptism and the Lord's Supper or Eucharist meet these requirements. Water is the external sign of baptism, and bread and wine constitute the external sign of the Supper. Both contain the promise of forgiveness of sins. This latter is the reason mainline Protestant churches do not practice footwashing as a sacrament even though Jesus *appears* to have commanded it. It does not contain a promise of forgiveness.

Christian Baptism

From the New Testament point of view, water baptism is not optional; it is the command of Jesus and the apostles. In the New Testament there simply were no unbaptized Christians; in fact, receiving Christ was almost automatically followed by baptism.

It was in the moment of baptism that the believer was making his confession to the world that "Jesus is Lord!" To be a New Testament Christian meant to believe in your heart and to confess with your mouth. This confession acknowledged the new creation. "What does it [the righteousness of faith] say? The word is near you, on your lips and in your heart (that is, the word of faith which we preach); because, if you confess with your lips that Jesus is Lord and believe in your heart that God raised him from the dead, you will be saved. For man believes with his heart and so is justified, and he confesses with his lips and so is saved" (Rom. 10:8-10, RSV).

In the sacramental theology of the Earliest Church as reflected in the New Testament documents, the Christian's baptism was seen to be an identification with Jesus' baptism, so that the meaning of His baptism by John was transferred to the believer's. This is the significance of Paul's words in Rom. 6:4: "We were therefore buried with him through baptism into death" (NIV).

Jesus' baptism bore a double significance: (1) It was a proleptic event anticipating the Cross. Since the words from heaven identified the event as His induction into the vocation of the Suffering Servant of Isaiah 53 (see commentaries), and the final outcome of that vocation was death, His baptism was in view of His passion. In a very real sense, it was the advance enactment of His crucifixion. (2) It also was the moment, symbolized by the descent of the dove, when Jesus received the Holy Spirit without measure as the Messianic Spirit-bearer.

Both meanings were seen by the early Christians as attaching to the baptism of believers. Baptism was in anticipation of death in the sense that it was a declaration of intent to put to death those marks of the old life contrary to Christ. This is why Paul's argument in Romans 6 is so powerful against continuance in sin after baptism: "Shall we go on sinning so that grace may increase? By no means! We died to sin; how can we live in it any longer? Or don't you know that all of us who were baptized into Christ Jesus were baptized into his death?" (vv. 1-3, NIV).

Paul is suggesting that if they understood the nature of their baptism, they would never raise the question about the possibility of further sin, free grace notwithstanding. The baptismal ritual of the *Discipline* of the Methodist Episcopal Church, South (1918), insightfully contains the following prayer that embodies this truth: "O merciful God, grant that the Old Adam in these persons may be so buried that the New Man may be raised in them. Amen. Grant that all carnal affections may die in them, and that all things belonging to the Spirit may live in them. Amen."

The Christian's baptism then is a dramatization of his faith, an acting out of his dying with Christ to sin and rising with Him to newness of life. It also pictures the washing away of his sins.

Baptism was, further, the believer's incorporation into the visible church. He was said to be "baptized into Jesus Christ" (Rom. 6:3), just as the Israelites were "baptized unto Moses" as they passed through the Red Sea (1 Cor. 10:2). As the Israelites came under the authority and direction of Moses at the Exodus, so those baptized into Christ came under His Saviorhood and Lordship.

Even more profoundly, Christian faith is acted out in baptism and signifies the actual incorporation of the believer into Christ's incarnate presence on earth, His living Body where the Spirit dwells. "For by one Spirit are we all baptized into one body, whether we be Jews or Gentiles, whether we be bond or free; and have been all made to drink into one Spirit" (1 Cor. 12:13).

When baptism is received as a New Testament sacrament, it is the climax of conversion. It is the signing and sealing of our new relationship to Christ. It dramatically portrays our personal identification with Christ in His death and resurrection and pictures the washing away of our sins; and, when our faith is New Testament faith, baptism is God's own sealing of us as members of the Body of Jesus Christ where all "drink into one Spirit."

The best historical evidence suggests that the mode of baptism in the Early Church was generally immersion. In the *Teaching of the Twelve Apostles*, the Church's earliest manual of discipline (about A.D. 125), trine immersion "in living water" was the recommended mode. The believer was immersed first in the name of the Father, then in the name of the Son, finally in the name of the Holy Spirit. If no stream of living water was at hand, a pool of water would suffice "and if no cold water, then warm." However, if no stream or pool was available, "let him be poured three times."

But while the mode is optional, baptism itself is not. In our modern pietistic and individualistic way of thinking, we assume we can "take it or leave it." Not so! To refuse baptism is to disobey the clear command of the New Testament. Of course, preaching the gospel of the Crucified is the primary task of any preacher (1 Cor. 1:17), but baptism is not an either/or proposition.

A word needs to be said regarding *infant baptism.* It is falsely assumed by some that the ceremony is only appropriate to a sacramentarian view of the sacrament. According to this view, baptism really washes away the guilt of original sin and imparts regenerating grace to the infant.

A view that insists on the necessity of personal faith necessarily entails *adult* baptism, it would appear. Based on this understanding, the whole concept of baptism is rejected as related to children who have not reached the "age of accountability." In lieu of baptism, dedication of children is practiced.

Wesleyan theology allows for the practice of infant baptism, however, without falling into the faulty position of sacramentarianism. Central to Wesleyan thought is the idea of *prevenient grace* that provides "atonement" for all who are incapable of personal response, including babies (see Rom. 5:18). In this context, infant baptism may legitimately be practiced if desired as a witness to the reality of grace mediated through God's prevenient mercy. In this sense it is no more or less "saving" than adult baptism.

The Lord's Supper

The Lord's Supper is the second New Testament sacrament. In the Early Church it was observed every first day of the week. Although these early Christians commemorated the Lord's death by this Supper every Sunday, we have no New Testament *commandment* to this effect. It simply says, "As often as ye eat this bread, and drink this cup . . ." (1 Cor. 11:26). It need not be every Sunday, but it should be often. By this means the first Christians not only kept fresh in their memory the death of Jesus for their sins but also through the celebration of the Supper realized the presence of their risen Lord who was still among them!

The Lord's Supper is the Church's way of remembering that its salvation is not by human works but by the broken body and shed blood of Christ. "And he took bread, gave thanks and broke it, and gave it to them, saying, 'This is my body given for you; do this in remembrance of me.' In the same way, after the supper he took the cup, saying, 'This cup is the new covenant in my blood, which is poured out for you'" (Luke 22:19-20, NIV).

But it is more than an act of remembering, it is a proclamation. "For whenever you eat this bread and drink this cup, you proclaim the Lord's death until he comes" (1 Cor. 11:26, NIV). We *preach* the death of Jesus for our sins, not only in "the message of the cross" (1:18, NIV), but also by eating the bread and drinking the cup of the Supper. Even if the sermon was poor on a given Lord's day, the early Christians always heard the true gospel in the sacrament of the Lord's Supper!

The Supper thus became *Holy Communion,* for as Christ was "preached" He was present among them: "The cup of blessing which we bless, is it not the communion of the blood of Christ? The bread which we break, is it not the communion of the body of Christ?" (1 Cor. 10:16). The word "communion" here is the Greek *koinōnia,* which really means "participation" (NIV).

The one thing that is decisive about the Eucharist was that it actualized the presence of the risen Lord. Gustav Aulen emphasizes this point in these words:

> The living Christ has always been present in the celebration of the Lord's Supper. It was so at the last meal in the upper room. It was so likewise at the meals which the risen Lord shared with his disciples according to the narratives in the Gospels and Acts and which may be regarded as an introduction to the celebration of the sacrament in the ancient church. The presence of Christ did not cease when the risen Christ no longer showed Himself to his disciples. The religious significance of the Ascension lies in the fact that now the Living Lord was raised above the limitations of time and space, and therefore could be with his own "always, to the close of the age." The Lord's Supper is the particular place where he has promised to meet his own.[1]

How the bread and wine mediate this presence has been a matter of debate among Christian traditions throughout the centuries. As Jesus passed the elements among His disciples on that memorable evening, He said of them: "This is my body"; "This is my blood." How the "is" is interpreted is the crucial matter.

From the earliest days of the postapostolic period there was a tendency to interpret the Divine Presence in *realistic* terms. The

---

1. *The Christian Faith,* trans. Eric H. Wahlstrom and G. Everett Arden (Philadelphia: Muhlenberg Press, 1948), 344-45.

equation between the physical substances and the body and blood of Jesus was taken quite literally. Ignatius quite straightforwardly declares that "the Eucharist is the flesh of our Savior Jesus Christ, which suffered for our sins and which the Father in His goodness raised."

Not only were the elements considered "holy," but they involve the ingestion of Jesus in what to us is an almost repulsive sense. A typical description of the results of participation is that the Eucharist is the "medicine of immortality," an antidote against death that enables us to live in the Lord forever. Many of the early fathers give witness to this understanding.

One of the issues that needs to be considered in trying to comprehend their thinking was their battle with Gnosticism. The Gnostics denied the material reality of Jesus' body and insisted that only a "spiritual" reality was worthy of divine things. Against this, the Christian thinkers urged the full humanity of Jesus, which involved a flesh-and-blood body, and used the reality of the Eucharistic elements to support their position.

In the Western church, this conception became dominant. It was brought to full expression by Cyprian and strongly supported by Augustine. To this "crass materialism" is given the term *transubstantiation*. The substance of wine and bread was literally transformed into the literal body and blood of Jesus. He is present in the Eucharist in a most *realistic* way.

Martin Luther, in the 16th-century Reformation, not only rejected some other abuses of the Lord's Supper but also rejected the idea of transubstantiation. His view is commonly called *consubstantiation*. Luther, too, insists on the real presence of Christ but "alongside of" or "under" the bread. It is not the bread and wine that impart salvation but the actualization by faith of the words that Jesus spoke at the institution of the meal: "Given [and] shed for you . . . for the remission of sins" (Luke 22:19-20; Matt. 26:28). Here is the promise that is one of the distinguishing marks of a sacrament.

This truth highlights Luther's emphasis that it is the Word that is primary. Even if the signs (bread and wine) are lacking, he says, response to the Word will bring salvation. That is, one might be saved without the sacrament but not without the Word.

John Calvin varies from Luther in his interpretation of how the presence of Christ is actualized in the Eucharistic feast. He rejects both transubstantiation and consubstantiation because they insist on the literal presence of Christ in (or under) the elements. He argues that to require this requires Christ to be literally in two places at once; but since Christ is in heaven, it is not required that He also be "in the bread." While he admits a mystery, he still confesses that somehow the sacrament elevates us into His presence. While this differentiation may somewhat mystify us too, it is clear that Calvin wishes to maintain the reality of Christ's presence mediated by the sacrament.

A further departure from the *realistic* interpretations is associated with the name of Ulrich Zwingli, who prefers to speak of the Eucharist as a *memorial.* By this he seems to imply that to participate is simply an enacted remembering of an event past. Should such observances become mere routine for the partakers, repeated enactments could dull the vividness of the remembering. The weakness of this explanation is that there is no necessary presence of the Lord. The term *memorial* suggests that the sacrament is no different from any other act of commemoration; its elements have a rather arbitrary connection with its meaning.

If the term *memorial* is interpreted in a biblical sense, it entails a far more profound meaning than that suggested by Zwingli, or at least the popular understanding of his position. This may be seen if we recall that the Eucharist is the Christian counterpart to the Jewish Passover. Paul says, "Christ our passover is sacrificed for us" (1 Cor. 5:7). The annual Jewish festival was an act of recalling the past; but more than that, it brings the Exodus into the present as a living reality. It was far more than a "Fourth of July celebration" when rightly observed. In a very real sense, the Exodus was *reenacted* in the "now" of life. In the same way the Eucharist functions both to keep alive the memory of the Atonement and to make it contemporary reality. Gordon Kaufman describes this understanding well:

> This commemoration is one of the foundational events of a community's life, and participation in it renews once again the living effectiveness of that past in this present. In vividly confronting the church with the historical basis and purpose of her existence, it establishes her afresh in her proper life, so she can take up again the work assigned her. Through this "memorial," then, what might otherwise have fallen back into the dead past is kept effectively at work as living memory, and the symbols carrying this meaning of the past become channels of life for the community.[2]

---

2. *Systematic Theology* (New York: Charles Scribner's Sons, 1968), 492.

Consequently, we rob ourselves and cut ourselves off from the living tradition from which the Church lives when we neglect the regular observance of this rite. Rich blessing and joy can be the lot of Christian believers in keeping the Lord's Supper central to their worship in a properly observed and *understood* way. It is another of God's appointed ways of proclaiming the gospel.

Suggested Additional Reading

Ole E. Borgen, *John Wesley on the Sacraments.*
Oscar Cullmann, *Early Christian Worship.*
Armor D. Peisker, "Sacraments," *Beacon Dictionary of Theology,* 465-66.
J. S. Whale, *Christian Doctrine,* chap. 7.

Epilogue

The Return of Christ

The return of Christ is one of several theological truths falling under the general heading of eschatology or "doctrine of last things." This area of theology includes the destiny of man and the world, including the Judgment and eternal rewards and punishments. These doctrines are particularly susceptible to becoming the subject of extravagant speculations, but authentic Wesleyan thought shies away from becoming involved in such. It holds to the facts of the case but is reticent to go beyond the clear teaching of Scripture.

In the past few decades, great interest in eschatology has emerged and occupied the attention of theologians from all traditions. There have been various reinterpretations of the whole idea of eschatology in addition to multitudes of theories of realistic eschatology among conservative Christians. It is probably the most popular doctrine in terms of public interest today among all the basic Christian beliefs.

Traditionally, writers of theology have had difficulty knowing where to place this area among the list of theological doctrines. Consequently, it has commonly been treated last in the theology books and, unfortunately, as somewhat of an appendix. The renewed appreciation for eschatology in this era has caused scholars to recognize that it is not an addendum that could just as well have been omitted; rather it is central to the Christian faith.

We are placing our treatment of the Second Coming as an epilogue, not because of a feeling that it is unimportant, but because in a brief treatment such as this it is impossible to place it where it really belongs in a systematic theology—namely, as an integral part of the whole of Christian theology. Every theological doctrine is informed by eschatology. Since the return of Christ is the beginning of the last events in earthly history, it seems feasible in the light of the foregoing conditions to make it the last thing in this introductory survey.

So we say that instead of being last, in the New Testament, eschatology is the first doctrine: "Now after that John was put in prison, Jesus came into Galilee, preaching the gospel of the kingdom of God, and saying, The time is fulfilled, and *the kingdom of God is at hand:* repent ye, and believe the gospel" (Mark 1:14-15, italics added). The Greek may be translated: "The kingdom of God is *here!*"

The Future Is Here!

In Jesus the Messiah, God's kingdom was already present. "But if I cast out devils by the Spirit of God, then the kingdom of God is come unto you" (Matt. 12:28). In the ministry of Jesus, God's heavenly reign was being inaugurated. The miracles that attended our Lord's ministry were signs of the inbreaking of God's kingdom. The powers of the age to come were already at work!

God's kingdom was present in Jesus the King! "Being asked by the Pharisees when the kingdom of God was coming, he answered them, 'The kingdom of God is not coming with signs to be observed; nor will they say, "Lo, here it is!" or "There!" for behold, the kingdom of God is in the midst of you'" (Luke 17:20-21, RSV). Jesus was not talking about some mystical kingdom "within" them but "among" them. If the Pharisees but had eyes to see, the Messianic King was standing in their very midst! They were looking for signs in the heavenlies because they refused to recognize the signs of His heavenly words and deeds.

The Kingdom was present in Jesus' person and ministry; it would come in power after His death and resurrection. This is surely what He meant when He announced during His ministry, "I tell you the truth, some who are standing here will not taste death before they see the kingdom of God come with power" (Mark 9:1, NIV).

Shortly before His ascension Jesus promised, "You will receive power when the Holy Spirit comes on you" (Acts 1:8, NIV). "When the day of Pentecost came, they were all together in one place.

Suddenly a sound like the blowing of a violent wind came from heaven and filled the whole house where they were sitting. They saw what seemed to be tongues of fire that separated and came to rest on each of them. All of them were filled with the Holy Spirit and began to speak in other [languages, marg.] as the Spirit enabled them" (2:1-4, NIV). Those present on that historic day indeed saw God's kingdom coming with power!

The Last Days

The amazed multitude who assembled to ask, "What does this mean?" received this answer from Simon Peter, God's inspired interpreter of the event: "These men are not drunk, as you suppose. It's only nine in the morning! No, this is what was spoken by the prophet Joel:

> "In *the last days*, God says,
>   I will pour out my Spirit on all people.
> Your sons and daughters will prophesy,
>   your young men will see visions,
>   your old men will dream dreams. . . .
> I will show wonders in the heaven above
>   and signs on the earth below, . . .
>   before the coming of *the great and glorious day*
>   *of the Lord.*
> And everyone who calls
>   on the name of the Lord will be saved."
>   *(Acts 2:15-17, 19-21, NIV)*

The words here italicized for emphasis show that the inspired apostle declares that "the last days" are the days that stretch between Pentecost (when the kingdom of God came with power) and "the great and glorious day of the Lord" (when the Kingdom will come in glory).

Such is the New Testament teaching. The kingdom of God—the eschaton—was *inaugurated* by Christ's first advent; it will be *consummated* when He returns on "the great and glorious day."

Jewish rabbis divided all history into two ages. The old age they regarded as the days before the Messiah and the new age as beginning with His appearance. The New Testament modifies this. It sees the two ages—the present evil age and the age to come—as overlapping between the first and second appearances of Christ.

The new age has dawned with Christ, but the old will continue until He returns in glory to judge the world and consummate His kingdom. As new men we have "tasted . . . the powers of the age to come" (Heb. 6:5, RSV) in the gift of the Spirit. The indwelling Spirit points to the future; through Him we have a foretaste of the glory that shall be revealed when Christ returns. "We ourselves, who have the firstfruits of the Spirit, groan inwardly as we wait eagerly for our adoption as sons, the redemption of our bodies" (Rom. 8:23, NIV).

The Return of Christ

We cannot think scripturally about the Second Coming until we have said the preceding. For the Christian community the Second Coming is "that blessed hope, [even] the glorious appearing of the great God and our Saviour Jesus Christ; who gave himself for us, that he might redeem us from all iniquity, and purify unto himself a peculiar people, zealous of good works" (Titus 2:13-14).

The Church of Jesus Christ is an eschatological community, awaiting the blessed consummation. "Our citizenship is in heaven. And we eagerly await a Savior from there, the Lord Jesus Christ, who, by the power that enables him to bring everything under his control, will transform our lowly bodies so that they will be like his glorious body" (Phil. 3:20-21, NIV).

"If Christianity be not altogether restless eschatology," Karl Barth says, "there remains in it no relationship whatever to Christ." It is only as we feel the incompleteness of our salvation and the surge of hope that the gospel of Christ produces and the Spirit reinforces, that we utterly depend upon Christ. Apart from the hope of the Resurrection, we are of all men most miserable. But we have hope. Not pious yearnings for some vague kind of immortality, but a confident expectation of Christ's return in glory! "In this hope we were saved" (Rom. 8:24, NIV). Blessed hope!

Moreover, "Everyone who has this hope in him purifies himself, just as he is pure" (1 John 3:3, NIV). The blessed hope is a purifying hope. Always and everywhere the second coming of Christ is a call to both activity and preparedness. It is never presented in a way to cater to the curiosity seeker. Preoccupation with "signs" and "charts" betrays the most fundamental affirmation of Jesus himself: "It is not for you to know the times or the seasons, which the Father hath put in his own power" (Acts 1:7).

The function of the future in biblical faith is to throw light upon the present. We who live from the midpoint of history (the Cross) already know the outcome; so we wait with active preoccupation with the *present* work of the Kingdom, knowing that however and whenever the Crucified Messiah brings in His kingdom, we will by faith be a part of it.

"Even so, come, Lord Jesus" (Rev. 22:20).

Suggested Additional Reading

H. Ray Dunning, "Rapture," "Dispensationalism," *Beacon Dictionary of Theology*, 437, 168.

Norman R. Oke, "Second Coming of Christ," *Beacon Dictionary of Theology*, 474-75.

Stephen Travis, *I Believe in the Second Coming of Christ*.

J. S. Whale, *Christian Doctrine*, chap. 8.

Glossary

ADOPTION. Term used to refer to the relation established at conversion between God and His children, by which they become "sons of God."

AGAPE. Greek word used by NT writers to refer to God's love. Conveys the idea of disinterested and outgoing concern in contrast to loving out of need or for purpose of self-satisfaction.

APOLLINARIANISM. Heresy that taught that Jesus has a human body and soul, but the spirit, mind, or logos of Christ's person was divine. He did not have a human mind.

ARIANISM. Heresy that said Christ was the highest and first of created beings. He was not eternal and thus not fully God but was just a creature.

ATONEMENT. Comprehensive term referring to the work of Christ (or sacrifices in the Old Testament) in its function of overcoming the estrangement between man and God.

DOCETISM. Taught that Christ only appeared to have a human body; the physical was illusory. Therefore He only *seemed* to suffer and die.

EBIONITISM. Teaching that Christ was only a man. He became the Messiah at His baptism by John; He did not become God at that time. It denied the Virgin Birth and rejected Paul's teachings.

ELECTION. Refers to God's activity in choosing persons for special tasks and His eternal purpose for men, namely, that they are to be holy in character and like Christ. Never used in the Bible to refer to a choice of eternal destiny.

ESCHATON. Refers to the final consummation or to a goal toward which history is moving. The eschaton for the Old Testament is the coming of the kingdom of God; this eschaton arrived in the first coming of Christ and His inauguration of the Kingdom. For the New Testament it is the second coming of Christ and the full and final consummation of the Kingdom.

EUTYCHIANISM. Ancient heresy that taught that Christ had one nature resulting from the mingling of the divine and human natures to the extent that the human nature was swallowed up by the divine. He had two natures before the Incarnation but only one afterward.

EXISTENTIAL. Literally refers to human existence and is almost synonymous with "personal." Used in this book to refer to a relationship between knower and known that determines the existence of the knower. It contrasts to mere intellectual knowledge and stresses the commitment of the whole person.

GNOSTICISM. Movement that became prominent in the second century that taught salvation by knowledge. One of its basic tenets was a dualism of spirit and matter with matter being evil. Salvation thus involved escape from the body.

IDOLATRY. The elevation of a finite object, ideas, or system to an object of worship.

INCARNATION. Literally means "en-flesh-ment." In Christian theology the taking on of human flesh by God in the person of Jesus Christ.

INSPIRATION. Primarily refers to the Holy Spirit "in-breathing" the biblical writers so that they speak with authority.

LOGOS. Greek term translated "word" in the Fourth Gospel. In philosophy it means structure or reason and refers to the nature of reality. It is the Christian claim that this logos has become incarnate (see above) in Jesus Christ.

MONOPHYSITISM. One nature. A Christological heresy exemplified by Eutychianism. Denies the two natures, divine and human, in Christ.

NESTORIANISM. The doctrine that Christ really had two personalities. They were housed in one body.

ONTOLOGICAL. Derived from *ontos,* meaning "being." Refers to the nature of reality, what a thing is.

PENANCE. Roman Catholic sacrament that resulted in the forgiveness of sins. Involved contrition, confession, and satisfaction leading to the word of absolution pronounced by the priest.

PIETISM. A movement that emphasized personal religious experience. Historically originated in the 17th century with Philipp Jakob Spener in Germany.

PREDESTINATION. Refers to God's purposes for man that He determined beforehand. In Scripture refers exclusively to the way of salvation in Christ and God's plan for the ethical life of His people, never with reference to God's deciding one's eternal destiny.

RECONCILIATION. Domestic figure of speech used to describe the results of the work of Christ. The estranged parties, God and man, are reunited through the Atonement.

REGENERATION. Theological term synonymous with *new birth.* Conveys the idea of bringing to life from the dead in terms of spiritual life.

RELIGION. Generally refers to an attitude of dependence by man upon something or someone greater than he. Defined by F. Schleiermacher as "a feeling of absolute dependence."

SACRAMENT. In Protestant theology a sacrament involves an outward sign accompanied by a promise of the forgiveness of sins. When received in faith, it becomes a means of grace. Protestants, on this view, accept only two sacraments: baptism and the Lord's Supper.

SACRAMENTARIANISM. View that the sacraments automatically bestow grace without respect to the moral qualifications or faith of the participants.

SALVATION. Literally means "to be free." General term referring to the total work of God restoring man to his right relation to the Divine.

Bibliography

Aulen, Gustav. *Christus Victor.* New York: Macmillan Co., 1945.

————. *The Faith of the Christian Church.* Translated by Eric H. Wahlstrom. Philadelphia: Fortress Press, 1960.

Baillie, Donald M. *God Was in Christ.* London: Faber and Faber, 1961.

————. *The Theology of the Sacraments.* New York: Charles Scribner's Sons, 1957.

Barclay, William. *The Daily Study Bible. Gospel of John,* Vol. 1. Philadelphia: Westminster Press, 1955.

————. *The Promise of the Spirit.* Philadelphia: Westminster Press, 1960.

Barth, Karl. *Dogmatics in Outline.* Translated by G. T. Thompson. London: SCM Press, 1957.

Berkhof, Louis. *The History of Christian Doctrines.* Grand Rapids: Baker Book House, 1976.

Bright, John. *The Kingdom of God.* New York: Abingdon Press, 1953.

Brunner, H. E. *Man in Revolt.* Translated by O. Wyon. New York: Charles Scribner's Sons, 1939.

Calvin, John. *A Compend of the Institutes of the Christian Religion.* Edited by Hugh T. Kerr. Philadelphia: Westminster Press, 1964.

Cannon, Wm. Ragsdale. *The Theology of John Wesley.* New York: Abingdon Press, 1946.

Carter, Charles W. *The Person and Ministry of the Holy Spirit.* Grand Rapids: Baker Book House, 1974.

Clarke, Wm. Newton. *The Christian Doctrine of God.* New York: Charles Scribner's Sons, 1909.

Cullmann, Oscar. *The Christology of the New Testament.* Translated by Shirley C. Guthrie and Charles A. M. Hall. Philadelphia: Westminster Press, 1959.

Dodd, C. H. *The Apostolic Preaching.* New York: Harper and Bros., 1962.

Flew, R. Newton. *Jesus and His Church.* London: Epworth Press, 1938.

————. *The Idea of Perfection in Christian Theology.* London: Oxford University Press, 1934.

Gould, J. Glenn. *The Precious Blood of Christ.* Kansas City: Beacon Hill Press, 1959.

Greathouse, W. M. *From the Apostles to Wesley.* Kansas City: Beacon Hill Press of Kansas City, 1979.

Hoekema, Anthony A. *The Bible and the Future.* Grand Rapids: Wm. B. Eerdmans Publishing Co., 1979.

Jones, E. Stanley. *The Way to Power and Poise.* Nashville: Abingdon-Cokesbury Press, 1946.

Kaufman, Gordon D. *Systematic Theology.* New York: Charles Scribner's Sons, 1968.

Kelly, J. N. D. *Early Christian Doctrines.* San Francisco: Harper and Row, Pub., 1978.

Ladd, George Eldon. *The Blessed Hope.* Grand Rapids: Wm. B. Eerdmans Publishing Co., 1956.

Lawson, John. *Introduction to Christian Doctrine.* Wilmore, Ky.: Francis Asbury Publishing Co., 1980.

Luther, Martin. *A Compend of Luther's Theology.* Edited by Hugh T. Kerr. Philadelphia: Westminster Press, 1974.

McKinley, O. Glenn. *Where Two Creeds Meet.* Kansas City: Beacon Hill Press, 1959.

Mackintosh, Hugh Ross. *The Doctrine of the Person of Christ.* New York: Charles Scribner's Sons, 1915.

Micks, Marianne H. *Introduction to Theology.* New York: Seabury Press, 1967.

Moody, Dale. *The Word of Truth.* Grand Rapids: Wm. B. Eerdmans Publishing Co., 1981.

Pinnock, Clark H. *Grace Unlimited.* Minneapolis: Bethany Fellowship, 1975.

Purkiser, W. T. *Interpreting Christian Holiness.* Kansas City: Beacon Hill Press of Kansas City, 1971.

Purkiser, W. T., et al. *Exploring Our Christian Faith.* Rev. ed. Kansas City: Beacon Hill Press of Kansas City, 1978.

Ramsey, A. M. *The Resurrection of Christ.* Philadelphia: Westminster Press, 1946.

Read, David H. C. *The Christian Faith.* Nashville: Abingdon Press, 1956.

Scott, E. F. *The Fourth Gospel.* Edinburgh, 1906.

Starkey, Lycurgus M. J. *The Work of the Holy Spirit.* Nashville: Abingdon Press, 1962.

Taylor, Richard S. *A Right Conception of Sin.* Kansas City: Nazarene Publishing House, 1939.

Taylor, Vincent. *Jesus and His Sacrifice.* London: Macmillan and Co., 1937.

Temple, William. *Nature, Man, and God.* London: Macmillan and Co., 1935.

Travis, Stephen H. *Christian Hope and the Future.* Downers Grove, Ill.: InterVarsity Press, 1980.

Wesley, John. *A Plain Account of Christian Perfection.* Kansas City: Beacon Hill Press of Kansas City, 1968.

————. *Standard Sermons.* Edited by Edward H. Sugden. 2 vols. London: Epworth Press, 1921.

Whale, J. S. *Christian Doctrine.* New York: Macmillan Co., 1941.

Wiley, H. Orton. *Christian Theology.* 3 vols. Kansas City: Beacon Hill Press, 1940-43.

Wiley, H. Orton, and Culbertson, Paul T. *Introduction to Christian Theology.* Kansas City: Beacon Hill Press, 1946.

Wright, G. Ernest, and Fuller, Reginald. *The Book of the Acts of God.* Garden City, N.Y.: Doubleday, 1960.

Subject Index

Adoption, 87
Apollinarianism, 35
Apostles' Creed, 38
Arianism, 30, 36
Atonement
  the act of God, 66
  extent of, 63-64
  moral influence theory, 63
  penal satisfaction theory, 63-64
  ransom theory, 62
  satisfaction theory, 62-63
Awakening, 83

Baptism
  adult, 111
  death to sin, 109
  infant, 111
    and prevenient grace, 111
  mode of, 110
  not optional, 109
  supposedly part of salvation, 99,
    111
Bible
  as holy, 11
  as source of doctrine, 15
  as witness to Christ, 14
Bibliolatry, 10

Chalcedonian Creed, 10, 33, 36
Christian ethics, 76
Christology
  New Testament, 29
  as paradoxical, 37
Church
  as the Body of Christ, 101
  as holy, 105
  as local congregation, 102
  mission of, 102
  as new Israel, 100, 106
  as new temple, 45
  as the people of God, 100
  and the Spirit, 103
  unity of, 104
  as universal, 105
  visible and invisible, 103
  Wesleyan definition, 105-6
Confession, 84
Consubstantiation, 113
Council of Constantinople, 40

Council of Nicea, 30
Creation, 26, 40

Day of the Lord, 43, 119
Divine Presence, 39, 45, 112-13
Docetics, 34

Ebionites, 34
Elohim, 25, 40
Eschatology, 117
Eutychianism, 36

Faith, 85
Footwashing, 108

General revelation, 21
Gnosticism
  and the Lord's Supper, 113
God
  existence of, 20-21
  holiness of, 11, 24
  knowledge of, 24
  as love, 26
  name of, 22-23
  as social Being, 25-26, 40
  Wesleyan view, 63-64
Gospel of Thomas, 34
Grace, 60 n
  Catholic view, 71
  objective, 73
  Pelagian view, 71
  subjective, 73
Growth in grace, 92

History
  as revelatory, 9-10
Holiness
  ceremonial, 90
  of God, 11, 24, 90
  as love for God, 25
  prophetic, 91
  as relation to God, 54

Image of God, 52
  ambiguity of, 53
  Catholic view, 71
  essential and existential, 53
  natural and moral, 53
  as a relation, 52-53
Infant baptism, 111
  and prevenient grace, 111

Internal testimony of the Holy Spirit, 10

Jehovah, 23
Jesus Christ
  and Adam, 55
  and creation, 31
  as King, 66-67
  as Logos, 29
  offices, 64
  preexistence, 30-31
  as Priest, 65
  as Prophet, 64-65
  as Revelation, 9, 28
  and the Spirit, 43
  as Suffering Servant, 29, 33, 109
  titles given to, 28-29
Judges (OT), 42, 44
Justification, 82, 86
  distinguished from sanctification, 91

Kingdom of God, 37, 44, 88, 118, 119

Last days, 119
Logos, 29, 30-31, 33, 35
Lord's Supper
  as memorial, 114
  Protestant view, 108
  supposedly part of salvation, 99

Man, attempts to define, 51-52
Means of grace, 107

Natural law, 31
Nestorianism, 35-36
New birth, 91-92
Nicene Creed, 10, 30, 33, 40, 46

Original sin, 54-55
  existential meaning, 56
  historical meaning, 55
  theological meaning, 55

Paradox
  and Christian experience, 37, 76
  and Christology, 37
Pelagianism, 57, 71-72
Penance, sacrament of, 84
Pentecost, Day of, 41, 44, 119
  birthday of the Church, 45, 103
Philosophy
  and God's existence, 19-20
Prevenient grace, 21, 60, 72, 111
  and infant baptism, 111
Primitive holiness, 54
Purgatory, 82

Qodesh, 90

Reconciliation, 86
Regeneration, 92
Repentance, 84
  Calvin's view, 85
  Wesley's view, 85
Revelation
  as historical, 9

Sacramentarianism, 107, 111
Sacraments
  Catholic view, 108
  Protestant view, 100, 108
Salvation
  corporate character, 88
  as divine-human encounter, 86-87
  order of, 82
Sanctification, 82
  Catholic view, 82
  distinguished from justification, 91
  entire, 93
    as instantaneous and gradual, 94-95
    as love, 93, 94
  initial, 92
  as real change, 91
Sin
  death to, 94-95, 109
  as enslavement, 57
  as self-sovereignty, 57-58
  Wesleyan view, 64
Special revelation, 21-22
Spirit
  and conversion, 46
  eschatological hope, 43
  and the Messiah, 43
  in the OT, 42
  and power, 44
  as Sanctifier, 47
  as Source of life, 46
Stoics, 29

Tetragrammaton, 23
Transubstantiation, 113
Trinity, 33, 39, 40

Unitarians, 32
Unitarianism, 35 n

Virgin Birth, 32-33

Westminster Catechism, 54

Yahweh, 23

Person Index

Abelard, 63
Anselm, 62
Apollinaris, 35, 36
Aquinas, Thomas, 71, 82, 83
Aristotle, 20
Arius, 30
Auber, Harriet, 76
Augustine, 32 n, 54, 71, 72, 73, 83,
    113
  on original sin, 58
  on the Spirit and the church, 104
Aulen, Gustav, 62, 67, 112

Baillie, Donald, 37, 76
Barclay, William, 31, 33
  on the Bible, 11
Baring-Gould, Sabine, 104
Barth, Karl
  on eschatology, 120
Bence, Clarence, 96
Browning, Robert, 37
Brunner, Emil, 53

Calvin, John
  on Atonement, 63
  on the Lord's Supper, 113-14
  on predestination, 72
  on repentance, 85
Cyprian, 104, 113

Diogenes, 51

Edwards, Jonathan, 76
Eutyches, 36

Ferré, Nels, 59

Graham, Billy, 54
Grensted, 59

Heracleitus, 20, 29
Hume, David, 20

Ignatius, 113
Irenaeus, 71, 71 n, 104

Jones, E. Stanley, 33, 44

Kant, Immanuel, 20
Kaufman, Gordon
  on the Lord's Supper, 114
Kierkegaard, Sören, 37

Luther, Martin, 68
  on grace and freedom, 72

on justification, 99-100
on justification and
    sanctification, 82
on the Lord's Supper, 113
on Scripture, 13
on sin, 58-59

Mackintosh, Hugh Ross, 34
Martyr, Justin, 71
Moody, Dwight L., 70

Nestorius, 35
Nietzsche, Friedrich, 31
Nygren, Anders, 94

Origen, 32 n, 71
Otto, Rudolf, 21

Pelagius, 57-58, 71
Plato, 20
Purkiser, W. T., 13

Ramsdell, Edward T., 55
Read, David H. C., 39, 45-46

Sartre, Jean-Paul, 54
Scott, E. F., 31
Scott, Walter
  on the Bible, 15
Spafford, Horatio G., 64

Temple, William, 31
Tertullian, 32 n, 36, 87
Twain, Mark, 51

Watts, Isaac, 41
Wesley, Charles, 47
Wesley, John, 53, 83
  on the Bible, 10
  on the divine and human
      working, 73
  on the divine nature, 63-64
  and Eastern thought, 87
  on entire sanctification, 93, 97
  on grace and freedom, 72
  on original sin, 56, 58, 72
  on prevenient grace, 60, 74-75
  on sin, 57
  and social religion, 99
Westcott, B. F., 97
Wiley, H. Orton, 13, 27, 96, 105
Williams, Colin, 94

Zwingli, Ulrich
  on the Lord's Supper, 114

Scripture Index

Genesis:
1:1   19, 25, 30
1:26   40
2:7   46
3:5   57
3:15   29
3:22   57
6:1-8   46
9:6   53
12   100
12:1-3   106
17:1   22
32:27, 28   22

Exodus:
3:14, 15   23
19:5-6   101
20:2-3   25

Leviticus:
17:11   66
19:2   25

Numbers:
11:29   42

Deuteronomy:
7:6   101
11:7   10

Joshua:
24   24

Judges:
5:11   10

1 Samuel:
3:9   14
10:6   42
12:7   10
19:23-24   42

Psalms:
14:1   19
53:1   19
85:10   27
106:2   10
139:8   53
145:4, 12   10
146:4   46
150:2   10

Proverbs:
8:23   31

Ecclesiastes:
12:7   46

Isaiah:
9:6   29
53   33, 109
53:2   33
53:6   29, 57
55:7   84
61:1-2   43

Ezekiel:
10   45
33:11   84
37:1-14   46
43:1-4   45

Joel:
2:28 ff.   43

Matthew:
3:8   84
4:4   14
12:28   118
18:20   45
20:28   62
22:34-40   25
23:17, 19   91
26:28   113

Mark:
1:14-15   118
9:1   118

Luke:
1:35   32
2:52   34
3:8   108
4:16-21   102
4:18-21   43
15   64
15:17-20   87
17:20-21   118
22:19-20   112, 113
23:42-43   84
24:25-27   14

John:
1:1   30
1:3   31, 32
1:13   32
1:14   30, 32
1:18   33
3:1-8   46

3:3 ff.   92
3:6   56, 59
3:16   30
5:39   14
6:37   85
7:17   33
7:37-39   43
14—16   43
14:23   40, 43
16:8   46
20:21   102

Acts:
1:1   102
1:7   120
1:8   118
2:1-4   119
2:15-17, 19-21   119
2:22   10
2:22-36   29, 38
3:12-26   10
7:48-50   45
16:31   73
17   21
17:22-24   21
17:24-25   25

Romans:
1:18-25   24
1:18-32   55
3:24-25   66
3:26   86
4   100
4:9-13   100
4:15   59 n
4:20-25   85
5   26, 65
5:1   68, 86
5:5   94
5:6   26
5:8   26
5:10   26
5:11   68, 86
5:12, 18   60
5:12-21   55
5:18   111
5:20   59 n
6   109
6:1-3   109
6:3   110
6:3-4   100

6:4   88, 109
7   56
7:7-13   59 n
7:9   59
7:14-25   56
7:24   56
7:25   57, 60
8:1   96
8:9-11   44
8:14-17   87
8:16   87
8:23   120
8:24   120
9:6   103
9:6-9   100
10:8-10   109
12:4-5   102
15:16   47

1 Corinthians:
1:2   92
1:17   111
1:18   112
1:21   21
3:16   45
5:7   114
6:9-11   92
6:15-17   102
10:2   110
10:16   112
11:26   111, 112
12:3   47
12:12-13   102
12:12-27   102
12:13   110
12:27   102
15:45   47

2 Corinthians:
3:18   47

4:4   88
5:17   88
5:18   66
5:19   33, 35, 65, 66
5:20   87
6:1   75

Galatians:
2:20   37, 68, 69
3:28   101
4:6-7   87
5:6   83
6:16   101

Ephesians:
1:3-7   67
1:22-23   101
2:1   74, 83
2:3   59
2:11-15   88, 101
2:11-22   22
2:18   47 n
2:19-22   45
3:16-19   44
3:19   48
4:4-6   101

Philippians:
1:6   74, 75, 96
2:5-11   38
2:12-13   73, 74
3:8   64
3:10   68
3:20-21   120

Colossians:
1:21-23   75
2:9   33, 40
2:9-23   101
2:15   67

1 Thessalonians:
5:16   96

2 Thessalonians:
2:13   47

1 Timothy:
2:5-6   35
3:16   34, 37, 38

Titus:
2:13-14   120

Hebrews:
1:1-3   9, 21
1:3   34
1:3-14   65
2:10   34
4:9-10   97
4:15   34
5:1-8   65
5:7, 8, 9   34
6:1   96-97
6:5   120

1 Peter:
1:1   100
1:10-12   14
2:9-10   22, 101

2 Peter:
1:16-21   10
3:18   92

1 John:
3:3   120
3:4   57
4:8   63
4:9   26
4:10   66
4:19   83

Revelation:
22:20   121

Other Books Written or Contributed to by William M. Greathouse

From the Apostles to Wesley
BF083-410-5888

The Fullness of the Spirit
BF083-410-2498

Romans
(Beacon Bible Expositions, Vol. 6)
BF083-410-3176

Sanctify Them . . . That the World May Know
BF083-411-2019

Other Books Written or Contributed to by H. Ray Dunning

Biblical Resources for Holiness Preaching, Vol. 1
BF083-411-3392

Biblical Resources for Holiness Preaching, Vol. 2
BF083-411-4658

Grace, Faith, and Holiness
BF083-411-2191

A Layman's Guide to Sanctification
BF083-411-3872

Order from your local bookstore, or call toll-free:

BEACON HILL PRESS OF KANSAS CITY
1-800-877-0700

CPSIA information can be obtained
at www.ICGtesting.com
Printed in the USA
BVHW081307160222
629192BV00001B/74